THE AUDITION BOOK

Winning Strategies for Breaking into Theater, Film, and Television

Ed Hooks

BACK STAGE BOOKS

An imprint of Watson-Guptill Publications, New York

This book is dedicated to my daughter,
Dagny,
who reacquainted me
with The Little Engine That Could.

Copyright © 1989 Ed Hooks

First published 1989 by Back Stage Books, an imprint of Watson-Guptill Publications, a division of Billboard Publications, Inc., 1515 Broadway, New York, NY 10036

Library of Congress Cataloging-in-Publication Data

Hooks, Ed.
    The audition book : winning strategies for breaking into theater, film, and television / by Ed Hooks.
        p.   cm.
    Includes index.
    ISBN 0-8230-7509-5
    1. Acting—Auditions.   2. Performing arts—Vocational guidance.
I. Title.
PN2071.A92H6   1989   89-31696
791'.023-dc20   CIP

Manufactured in the United States of America

First printing, 1989

1   2   3   4   5   6   7   8   9   /   94   93   92   91   90   89

Acknowledgments

Suddenly, you find yourself on stage, and you're happy there are others there with you. My thanks to Bob Bancroft for helping me find my voice, Fred Weiler for not letting me use it too much, Janet Rotblatt, Sam Mitnick, Beverly Long, Lynda Gordon, Jim Fox, Mark Locher, Dennis Danziger, Marie Salerno, Jean Shiffman, and especially Cally.

Contents

Foreword by Richard Thomas   *vii*

Introduction   *1*

PART ONE • AUDITIONING BASICS

1   Audition Anxiety and What to Do About It   *7*

2   Audition Guidelines   *14*

3   Casting Directors   *20*

PART TWO • AUDITIONING

4   Auditioning for TV Commercials   *29*

5   Auditioning for Voice Work   *55*

6   Auditioning for TV Shows   *62*

7   Auditioning for Movies   *78*

8   Auditioning for Industrial/Educational Films   *88*

9   Auditioning for the Stage   *94*

   PART THREE • THE BUSINESS SIDE OF ACTING

10 Managing Your Acting Career   *107*

11 Finding and Keeping an Agent   *111*

12 Theatrical Photos and Resumes   *124*

13 Performers' Unions   *134*

14 "What Do *You* Think?"   *137*
    Questions and Opinions

    Conclusion   *143*
    Appendix   *145*
    Glossary   *149*
    Index   *161*

Foreword

If one function of the critic is to remind us that we are entitled only to our labor and not necessarily the fruits thereof, it is possible that auditions exist to remind us that we may not even be entitled to the work.

I have been auditioning for thirty-one years so far—from the ages of seven to thirty-eight—and one thing I've learned is that, just like our chroniclers in the press, the business of going after the job is here to stay.

Even when you're no longer auditioning in the most conventional sense—taking your dignity and talent in hand and giving it your best shot in front of strangers—you're still being auditioned. Your last piece of work is being analyzed for its critical/financial success or failure. Your physical qualifications for a role are being considered. People are even asking if you're good to work with or a pain in the neck. And, in these situations, you frequently don't even get the chance to show them what you can do.

Many is the actor who, after years of success and popularity, finds himself not only in the position of being required to go after a role, but feeling with his heart that he *wants* to go after it. That he *must* have it. That he and only he can truly bring it to life. Then, if he lands the job, he feels the exhilaration of knowing he can still hold his own against all comers, that he is, in fact, not only in the profession he loves most, but in the one he deserves to call his own.

This may be the most salutary psychological aspect of the painful, nerve-wracking process of the audition. It serves to remind us of how privileged we are when we get to do what pleases us the most—perform.

As actors, we live much of our professional lives in a posture of supplication: ''Please, may I have permission to act?'' ''Please, may I take another second to prepare for this close-up?'' ''Please, can we go through this bit again? I don't quite seem to have it yet.'' But most of all, ''Please appreciate me. Please like me.'' The art we perform is a service, and so we aim to please. Most importantly we must please ourselves through the work. But the fact is, if we don't please others as well, we'll eventually get the hook.

The good news is that we're all in the same boat. We're all ''on the street'' in some measure, and it is this sense of a shared experience that gives the book in your hand its warmth of tone, its qualities of reassurance and unsentimental pragmatism.

Ed Hooks knows whereof he speaks—and he speaks well. His ability to organize our ideas about a process which can, at the wrong moment, turn even the most seasoned professional into a histrionic pudding, allows us to draw a clear bead on the target and helps us all to take those necessary deep breaths.

Yes, it seems unfair. Yes, there are too many people after the same job. Of course, the folks you read for can be not only hopelessly unimaginative, but callous as well. And yes, most of the actors who get the jobs you wanted can't hold a candle to your shining talent. Yes, yes, yes! Well, all this and fifty cents will get you a very bitter cup of coffee. You want to get up on the wicked stage? Get in line and sing for your supper.

This book is full of things you should know, and also good advice on what you should do—and there's nothing high-falutin' about it. The underlying philosophy is, of course, use what's best for you and do what you need to do to get the job. But the method of the book—its categorizing and specific nature—keeps it from being a useless, generalized pep talk.

I have only auditioned once for a commercial—when I was about nine or ten years old. It was for a well-known national bus line, and I didn't get the job. The people doing the casting very kindly took my parents aside and told them that, though I seemed to be a nice enough boy with the right qualifications, unless I had the birthmark (their term was "blemish") removed from my left cheek, I probably wouldn't get much work. It was decades later when I finally did make a commercial, but that's another story. The point is, I don't know beans about commercial auditions, and if my parents had listened to those folks, someone with a "blemish" would now be getting all my jobs. The advice Ed Hooks gives about this metier comes from long and fruitful experience, and I learned a great deal from him here.

I know a bit more about auditioning for roles in the theater, television, and film. But the sheer volume of common sense and information in this book gives me pause. Maybe, if I'd known there was so much to deal with, I wouldn't have tried. The answer, of course, is: Put the facts to use! Use your head. God knows, as soon as you hit the ground running and give that reading, you'll be using your heart for all it's worth. Method is essential. Your tank may be filled with the high octane of your talent, but you still have to drive the car. When I read this book, I felt it could help us all to keep our hands on the wheel.

I always look at dramatic auditions as a chance to act. I find that there is much more of an opportunity to use the technique of acting in an audition than we normally assume. In fact acting is, theoretically at least, something we're qualified to do. So if one treats the dramatic audition as a piece of work in itself, one is at least on familiar ground. You may not get the job, but you're focused on the work, the scene, your partner, not just on "how you're doing." In fact I see a lot of acting in theaters (particularly waiver theaters) which looks more like auditioning than the real thing. It's focused solely on the performance (not the technique of getting through the performance) and not really on the role or the text. In fact, it seems to be focused on the actor and his Self. Having sat many times on the "safe" side of the audition table, I can tell you that the more involved you are in the business of playing the scene, the more naturally your own qualities as a performer emerge.

All this has to do with fear, and fear, as Eleanor Duse once told a gifted young colleague, is vanity—the vanity of wanting to please, the vanity of fearing to fail. Auditioning can be a fearsome business. So the most important thing is to *do*, to *act*, to *be* what we have told ourselves we are, what we must *know* we are if anyone else is to believe in us. And then, all will be well; and with any luck and talent, we'll land the role.

In the meantime, thank heaven (and Ed Hooks) we have this book, with its humor, its knowledge, its accessibility. It is for all of us at some level, and it's written by a pro, one who not only wants us to get a callback—he wants us to get the job.

I can almost hear Ed Hooks saying, "Congratulations!"

RICHARD THOMAS
Hartford, Connecticut
April, 1989

Introduction

We are auditioning in one way or another for most of our lives: first as children crying for Mom's attention, later for that perfect after-school job, then for the favors of a lover. We audition for the limited spaces in the best colleges; for the rungs of the corporate ladder; for the basketball team, the cheerleading squad, and, if we go into politics, for votes. Someone even made a bumper sticker out of it: "Life is a constant audition."

You'd think, therefore, that actors would sort of accept auditioning for roles as a matter of course, that the procedure would be something life has at least mentally prepared us for. Unfortunately, that's not the case. The most sensitive and talented actor may be perfectly lousy in audition, rarely getting the opportunity to work at his craft, and the most mediocre performer may be supremely adept at pushing the buttons of the producers and directors, managing to merely muddle through the performance once he is hired.

If you want to be a professional actor, you have two major decisions to make: (1) you are going to be an artist rather than merely a device for a playwright to speak through, and (2) you are going to be paid. The suffering and broke artist who is living in a cold-water flat is a bad joke. There is no virtue in destitution. You don't become a better person because of it, and you certainly don't become a more talented artist. As an actor, the product you are putting into the marketplace is you and your sensibility, and that has a value that can be measured in monetary terms as well as human ones. The distinction really isn't between those who audition well and those who don't, but rather between those who intend to be paid and those who aren't convinced their skills are worth the money. There is a big difference between auditioning for a role in your church play and a role in the next Neil Simon play on Broadway—money.

In the professional theater, people get paid to do what they did for free in high school. Yet many individuals cross from amateur to professional status without really thinking about this fact. They know it, but they don't name it. Suddenly, the stakes are higher, the competition is searingly hot, and your confidence is put to the test. If you are doubtful about your place in the professional arena, you will pull your punches in audition, and you won't get cast. In this business, more than in any other I can imagine, self-doubt will sink your boat. If you are not absolutely convinced that you are the best one for the role, that there is a value to be placed on what you are doing, I guarantee they will not cast you. Call it arrogance if you want, but it is the defining characteristic of actors who work.

The accepted wisdom among professional actors is that the real job is the search for work; the actual acting is the fun part. That is why we are always on our way to an audition. Yet to say that we audition a lot doesn't tell the whole story, because contrary to popular belief, auditioning is not a generic activity. Those of us who make our livings at this know that it would be insanity to try the same techniques at an audition for a stage play that we use for commercials. You don't do the same things when auditioning for an industrial film that you do for a feature film, and auditions for voice jobs are different from all of the above. This perspective is what led me to write this book. I decided there is value in a real-world examination of the different kinds of auditions an actor might get in the course of a week. It is my aim to highlight the ways the auditions are similar and to contrast the ways these auditions differ.

My personal background allows me to shine a rather broad light on this subject: twenty years in New York and Hollywood, working as an actor, teacher, and occasional casting director. I've acted on the New York stage, in regional theater and stock, in films, and on television shows. My on-camera commercials number upwards of 150, many for leading national advertisers, and I've acted in countless industrial/ educational films. For thirteen years, I have conducted professional-level workshops in acting and audition technique.

I've looked at the process from every conceivable angle over a long period of time and in all media; I've been on both sides of the table, and have learned that auditioning is a skill that can be mastered. There is much that an actor should be doing if he wants to get hired consistently, and there are many pitfalls to avoid. However, the last thing I want to do is lure the unsuspecting innocent into this field. Acting is a devilishly difficult way to make a living, and, as the old saw goes, ''if there is any way you can avoid doing it, do so.'' I don't want to suggest that by reading this book, a novice can breeze right through the glittering gates of stardom, because it just isn't so. However, if the die is cast, or if you are already involved in the pursuit of an acting career and want to improve your averages, I believe this perspective will be useful to you.

The book is divided into three sections. The first two explore the auditioning process, discuss what the various kinds of auditions have in common and what they don't, and offer step-by-step ways to prepare for each. The third part of the book addresses the unavoidables that must be dealt with in order to get to the auditions in the first place, such as getting an agent and good photographs and joining the unions.

The fact that actors spend so much time in pursuit of work is illustrated by a story I heard Richard Benjamin tell back when he was first coming to prominence as an actor. After reading for the movie *Goodbye, Columbus*, he smiled, thanked the people, and turned to leave the room.

"Wait," the director called after him. "You are exactly what we want for the part. We need to talk about your availability."

"Pardon me?" responded Benjamin.

"We want to hire you for the picture."

"Oh, no," said the actor. "You must be making a mistake. I only do auditions."

And so it seems for us all. In fact, I think I hear my agent calling now.

PART ONE

AUDITIONING BASICS

1

Audition Anxiety and What to Do About It

Auditioning produces stress 100 percent of the time. It comes with the turf, and any actor who tells you otherwise is lying to you. No matter how many times you go through it, you never get used to it, never reach the point where you squeal with delight at the prospect of getting to show your stuff one more time. As your career develops, the stakes only get higher, the stress greater.

More bad news: auditioning is here to stay. Despite the coming of the computer age, there is simply no better way to match actors to roles. The process can't be automated and, until you become a bona fide star, you're just going to have to live with it. Even then you may not escape. Legend has it that Marlon Brando had to audition for *The Godfather* because the producers just couldn't imagine him as a Mafia boss, and he certainly had long since established himself as an international star.

And now the sunshine: stress can be managed in such a way that it won't interfere with your auditions. I won't go so far as to suggest that you will be unaware of it, but you can learn to work with stress so at least it doesn't ruin your readings. At times, you can even use it to your advantage.

THE SYMPTOMS OF AUDITION ANXIETY

We all know the symptoms: cotton mouth, tight throat, clammy hands, and rigor mortis of the lips. You might tremble and twitch a little, perspire profusely, have muscle spasms in your back. Worst of all is how difficult it is to concentrate. Once you are aware of your tension, it tends to be the only thing you can think about. Trying to put it out of your mind is like trying not to think of a black duck. And, of course, tension breeds tension, so the whole thing can escalate.

A few years ago, I participated in some screen tests for a new TV series being cast at 20th Century-Fox. My job was to commit two scenes to memory and then play both with each of the six finalists for the lead role in the show. We were on one of the soundstages on the Fox lot, and the contenders were kept waiting in motor homes in a nearby parking area. One by one, they were escorted onto the stage, introduced to me, and given the basic blocking of the scenes.

These were men who, by anybody's standards, would be considered successful. Perhaps they weren't superstars, but they were certainly recognizable from other TV shows, stage appearances, and, in one case, from a singing career. If you saw them, you would think they already had it made. Therefore, I was surprised to watch every single one of them struggle with tension. It was understandable that a new actor in town might be nervous in that situation, but these guys had been around. Still, it took hours to get through the tests because of botched takes, false starts, and too-sweaty faces.

What was going on? Why weren't they confident? Because—now think about this—if you get your own TV series, it is a career turning point, a shortcut to a Beverly Hills address and financial independence. All of the performers knew this, knew they were being scrutinized by network executives, producers, and agents, knew that this might be the best shot they would ever get. So the tension on the set could be cut with a knife.

P.S. When it was all over, who do you think got the part? In true Hollywood fashion, it wasn't even one of the nervous contenders. The role went to a fellow who had been nominated for an Academy Award a few years back. I don't think he auditioned, but I can't be sure. Anyway, the series went on the air, lasted six episodes, took a nosedive in the ratings, and is history. Next case.

It is a well-documented fact that fear number one for *all* people, whether they are actors or not, is having to get up in front of a group and make a speech. There is something inherently unnerving in the transaction. What are they thinking? Am I making sense? Do I look like a nervous wreck? Why aren't they smiling? Where's the exit?

Actors have it even worse, because not only do we have to get up in front of a group and do something, but the specific purpose that got the group together in the first place is to carefully scrutinize our delivery and style. It is very easy to take the position that you are being tested personally, and as soon as you do that, you're dead.

Audition anxiety is a sister of stage fright, and its causes are wrapped up in an actor's personal context as well as the importance of the project at hand. If you are feeling good about yourself in general, you will approach everything you do, including auditions, with more confidence than if you are feeling vulnerable or depressed. If there is a new love in your life, you will carry the euphoria right into the audition room with you; if you have had a string of acting jobs, you're bound to approach this one with confidence. On the other hand, if you haven't worked in six months, that anxiety can cause you to be off-balance, throwing off your timing.

All animals, including human ones, are designed to either fight the thing that threatens them or to run from it. But an actor in audition can do neither. He has to stand there with his feet in the fire and try to remain vulnerable to the text. He can't very well pick up a chair and throw it at the producer, and if he runs screaming from the room, he surely won't get cast.

At least part of the answer lies in changing the way we view the threat. Think about this: suppose everyone in the audition room was a close friend or relative. Would you still be nervous? Suppose the audition was taking place in your living room at home. Would you still be nervous? Suppose everyone in the audition room except you was eight years old. Would you still be nervous? Why not? What's the variable? You guessed it. In an actual professional-level audition, we are dealing with all unknown factors. We don't know the people who are watching our audition; we don't know whether or not we are on target with our work; we don't know for certain what they are thinking when they watch us; we don't know if we are up against Robert De Niro or Meryl Streep for the role. In short, we are on their turf, doing things on their terms.

But is there *really* a threat in the audition process? From having sat on both sides of the table, I am certain that most of the danger is a figment of the actor's extremely vivid imagination. The people watching truly want you to do well, want you to get the role. They take no pleasure in seeing you suffer and, if there was something they could think of to ease the tension, they'd do it. Most of the time, they are as uncomfortable about the process as the actors are.

SELF-FULFILLING PROPHECY

All actors need to go back and reread Dale Carnegie's book about winning friends and influencing people. What a smart man he was! He had a grasp on the concept of self-fulfilling prophecy before there was even a name for it.

In a nutshell, self-fulfilling prophecy means that you will tend to succeed if you think you will, and you will tend to fail if you think you will. The proposition has been stated and restated in countless forms: ''when you're hot, you're hot,'' ''money seeks money,'' ''them what's got, gets,'' ''on a roll,'' and so on. The point is that success breeds success, and this is never truer than in the audition room.

Put yourself in the position of the auditors. They have built this incredibly expensive race car, and they are looking for someone to drive it. They don't want to hire a person who comes in and fumbles around apologetically while hunting for the ignition. They don't want someone who has never driven a race car before. No, what they want is a winner, and a winner is someone who is already winning, not someone who plans to start winning next week.

"But, I'm new at this!" I can hear you protest. "How can I be expected to behave like a winner if I've never done this before?" Well, it comes down to the way you view the problem. Is the glass on the table half-full or half-empty? What is your personal policy in life? Do you normally expect to succeed at what you do? If so, why sould an audition room be different? Before you go into the audition room, you know all of the requirements, right? You may have taken some classes in audition technique, and you probably have been through at least a few cold reading situations. Trust that knowledge. Let it give you strength. You may never have seen a race car quite like the one these guys have built but, hey, if you can drive one, you can drive them all.

Think for a minute about the dynamic of a successful actor. He's not going to be overly concerned with what the auditors want to see; instead, he will show them how the role will be played if they use him. It's basic.

In my desk at home, I have a study done by a psychologist at Carnegie Mellon University in Pittsburgh. In it, he measured the practical impact of an optimistic versus a pessimistic attitude. First, he invented a standardized test that would categorize individuals as optimistic or pessimistic. Then, he began applying variables to each group to measure how they reacted to life's little failures. He tested reactions to such things as being late for an appointment or not getting a date with a desired person. What he discovered was that the individual with an optimistic attitude would invariably attribute failure to circumstances outside his immediate control and would plunge back in to try again; the pessimistic ones saw failures as signs of their own shortcomings, their own inadequacies, the realities of life, and they would tend to withdraw.

Then—and this is the fascinating part—the doctor took this same test and administered it to a bunch of insurance salesmen, people who face rejection every working day. The results were stunning and have major implications for actors. The optimistic group of salesmen sold 37 percent more insurance in their first two years on the job than their pessimistic counterparts! And, what is more, the pessimists were twice as likely to quit in their first year of employment.

A winning attitude is simply essential for actors in auditions. I'm not suggesting that you have to leap into the room grinning and glad-handing everybody, but if you don't think you ought to get the job, they won't either. At the professional level of acting, it is like going out every time and playing Jimmy Connors or Steffi Graf. Everybody is wonderful, and a few are downright brilliant. Winning the game, i.e., getting cast, can come down to nothing more than who most expects to win.

Again, put yourself in the position of the auditors. How would you respond if an actor meekly entered the room and tried really hard not to make any mistakes in his audition? Would you be impressed? Would you want him to drive your half-million-dollar race car? No, of course not. Remember this, write it on your bathroom mirror: *the avoidance of failure is not the same thing as the pursuit of success.* When you go into an audition, step out boldly, give the auditors something to choose. Don't worry that you will make mistakes that will cost you the job. I mean, you already don't have the job, right? You might as well try something because, in reality, you have nothing to lose.

SOME PRACTICAL EXERCISES

Stress in auditions is undoubtedly caused by mental attitude more than anything else, and the best remedy is going to be mental. You need to learn that you cannot relax by ordering yourself to do so. There is no gain in saying to yourself, ''I must not be nervous!'' because it will just have the opposite effect. Take a lesson from Masters and Johnson and their studies on male impotence. If a man is nervous and can't perform, the way to solve the problem is to shift his thinking to something positive, namely the pleasure at hand. If he dwells on his nervousness, he'll *never* perform!

Even if you don't feel like it, and you probably won't, go ahead and smile. Make yourself. Go into the bathroom and laugh at your silly self in the mirror. Laughter relaxes you immediately.

Don't just sit there in the chair in the waiting room and fret, physicalize. Go out in the hallway or outside the building and do something physical. Make some noise. Do jumping jacks, breathe in some deep breaths. Nervous actors are always forgetting to breathe. And don't worry that a producer or director or someone will see you jumping around in the hall. They already think actors are about a quart low anyway.

Try some tongue twisters. My favorite is this combo: ''The Swiss wrist watch sank swiftly'' and ''Peter Piper picked a peck of pickled peppers.'' Try saying them back to back. Gently slap your cheeks, pucker your lips, force the blood back into your lips. When you are tense, circulation to the extremities drops. This is why your hands are cold. By doing this exercise, you are kind of jump-starting your body. The principle is that if you can force circulation into your lips, it will help the rest of you relax.

Rehearse success. Boy, is this important, and it is directly related to self-fulfilling prophecy. I do it while en route to auditions. Imagine that you are a fly on the wall at the upcoming audition, and watch yourself go through the entire process as a winner. Watch as you enter the audition room, smiling and full of confidence. See how warmly the auditors respond to you? See how interested you are in them? Watch them relax with you as they realize that you are comfortable with this race car. When the director or casting director gives you some adjustments, watch yourself accept them with humor. After the audition is completed, watch yourself leave the room as the auditors smile. Feel the warmth of goodwill and approval.

Picture the auditors sitting there naked. I'm including this little gem because I've heard it about a hundred times. I'm not sure it works, but the idea is cute, and it might get you to smile.

2

Audition Guidelines

PLAYING A CHARACTER

There is a lot of confusion out there about playing a character, and I attribute it primarily to misinformation about the craft of acting. Every time I read an interview with some hot property who explains how he "becomes the character," I cringe because I know another five thousand aspiring actors just got the wrong idea.

I get people in my classes all of the time who think that acting is about "becoming a character," and they keep waiting for some kind of out-of-body experience. "When I'm a character," goes the logic, "I'm not myself." So, in order to construct a character, the first thing they want to do is layer on an accent or a trick voice or something. Of course, what they wind up with is closer to a caricature than a character.

The truth is that it takes time to develop an intelligent characterization—days, weeks, maybe even months. It isn't something you pull out of a hat at an audition. It involves a close study of the role and hopefully includes a rehearsal process in which you try different approaches, attempting to find the parts of yourself that might have evolved like the character you are going to play. Acting is not about hiding behind a character; it is about exposing yourself through one. When you are doing it well, it feels dangerous, not safe.

The best way to approach an audition is to take a long, cool look at what the scripted character is saying and doing in the scenes you will be reading—and accept whatever is going on there as *your* behavior. Don't waste time denying that you would behave or speak the way the he does. Immediately embrace it, and then get busy trying to justify it. The mistake occurs when an actor says, "Let's see . . . I, of course, would never behave like this. . . . What kind of character would behave in this silly fashion? Hmmmmm. . . ." Immediately, he's in trouble, because he has locked himself into the impossible task of assembling something purely from external factors.

"But, I would never, not in a million years, talk and behave like the person in this script!" you complain. Oh, yes you would, and yes you will, just as soon as you get into the audition room. Those very words are going to come right out of your mouth, so you might as well motivate them. There is no gain in denial.

At least part of the confusion comes from the cavalier way the term "character" is bandied about in commercials. I have heard very knowledgeable people advise new actors that they should have "two or three stock characters" for use at commercial auditions. And it is common to hear a casting director ask for "a really fun character." (In some commercials, you get to play non-human characters such as a dancing sock or a pickle or a grape, and the ad agency will even send cartoon renderings of the cuddly creatures to the audition.)

The problem is that people who work in advertising are not really part of the entertainment world at all, and they understand very little about an actor's craft. Their job is to sell products, period. Like most non-actors, they perceive that an actor "becomes a character," stepping outside of himself and changing into someone or something else. They don't know how we do what we do, only that we do it, and when they ask us for a character at an audition, they think that's a constructive direction. A new actor, one who doesn't have much training, will hear that kind of direction and try to do it, rather than translate it into something that is playable.

I once saw a casting director in a commercial workshop reduce a young actor practically to tears by insisting that he render a particular piece of copy as a "Bob Newhart character." The poor guy tried, and she would just shake her head, interrupting him with "No, that's not it. Try again." Finally, she sighed deeply and said, "Well, I guess you just can't do it." Totally depressed, now convinced that maybe he wasn't cut out to be an actor, he took his seat. After class, I sought him out and explained that the fault was not his, that it is impossible to render a Bob Newhart character. You can't be Bob Newhart—you can impersonate him, maybe, but that's not what the casting director was after. He was in a lose-lose situation because she was unable to enunciate what she really wanted. The only thing he could have done in the face of direction like that was to perhaps try to motivate a befuddled reading, because Newhart sometimes comes off that way. It might have satisfied her, but I doubt it.

Creating character voices for cartoons or radio commercials is another matter entirely, because you are not being seen. The key is that you are creating illusion, the sound of a character, not trying to portray one on-stage, and that is a different craft. Indeed, performers in this field frequently do have a stable of stock "characters," but if you watch them in the recording studio, you know in an instant that the process should not be confused with what an actor does in developing a characterization in other media.

Am I suggesting that every role you read for be reduced to a rendering of you and your everyday personality? Of course not. I'm only saying that it is a mistake to approach any scripted character with the attitude that you must step outside of your own skin in order to step into his. You have to find a way to express the character through yourself truthfully. Acting is not about hiding.

One last note on this subject, regarding the use of accents in auditions. The best policy is to use them only if absolutely necessary. If you are up for the part of an English barrister or a Jamaican singer, by all means try an accent. Otherwise, stick with standard American speech. And, whatever you do, don't confuse an accent with "character."

COSTUMING FOR AUDITIONS

There is open debate among actors regarding the wisdom of extreme costuming for an audition. If you are up for the role of a bag lady, should you wear something from Goodwill and bring the shopping cart?

Personally, I draw the line at really extreme costuming. I got my baptism in New York, where actors have to get around on the subways and it is impractical to lug costume changes. What you are wearing when you leave your apartment in the morning is what you will wear all day. In Hollywood, on the other hand, actors can toss their entire wardrobe in the trunk of the car, and many do.

One of my closest friends is a big devotee of costuming, and he recently went to an audition at Universal dressed up like Carmen Miranda, complete with high heels and lavish eye makeup. (I love to think of how far he would have gotten on the New York subways.) He didn't get the part, but I'm not going to argue with him about his dress. People who go in for this extreme stuff swear by it. They claim it helps them make a commitment to the role, and it lets the producers see exactly what they are going to get without having to use a lot of imagination. Pick your poison.

This is not to say that you can't wear shorts to a tennis-player audition or a swimsuit if they ask for one. No, I'm talking about dressing up like a Dickens character or an infantryman. The best policy in my book is a kind of safe middle ground: flexible clothing.

Swimsuit auditions, by the way, are a special kind of trauma, and if you think there is any chance at all you might get one, by all means invest in something flattering. The usual procedure is to wear the swimsuit under your street clothes when you go to the audition. There is less leering than you might imagine; it sort of takes the mystery out of things to have fifty imperfect bodies parading around under strong lights.

YOUR PHYSICAL APPEARANCE

With hair, moderation and flexibility are the keys. It is entirely possible to have an audition for a commercial in the morning and another audition for a period drama in the afternoon. You want to have a hair length and style that will cover both possibilities. Medium-length hair is best for adult men and women, but young girls and teens can get away with long hair. However you cut it, make sure it doesn't fall in your face when you move around. If they can't see your face, they won't cast you.

Hair color is a personal matter, and the only advice I have to offer is to make sure it looks authentic if you elect to color it. Also, if you are grey before your time, you might want to get rid of the grey. Agents and casting directors see grey hair and immediately put you into an older category. We're starting to see some aging Yuppies with salt and pepper hair, and that might be a harbinger of things to come. If that is you, I don't think I would change it. My concern is with those folks who are certifiably prematurely grey.

A note to men regarding mustaches: if you are wearing one because you think it makes you look older, odds are that you should shave it. If you have one of the Clark Gable/Tom Selleck variety, it might be okay. Generally speaking, facial hair in commercials is a no-no, but it isn't a restriction on TV shows, in movies, or on stage.

If you wear a hairpiece, for God's sake get a good one. Don't scrimp. If someone can tell by looking at you that you are wearing a piece, it is a bad piece. And remember, no one is going to volunteer that judgement. You have to be objective about yourself.

Makeup for women is a touchy subject. I see plenty of awful makeup in my classes, and I usually advise a couple of hours with a professional makeup consultant. It could be well worth the money. What looks swell when walking around the shopping mall in Boise might not fly at all in New York or Hollywood.

Teenage girls who have been through the modeling schools need to be particularly careful. The schools may be excellent, and they may teach you how to put on makeup, but too many teenagers use makeup to try to propel themselves into an older category. If you are in your teens, your money is almost surely in roles that call for the fresh and youthful look, and less makeup is better than more. I would say that if you are wearing so much that it is readily noticeable, it's too much. Do not take your role models from ''Dynasty'' reruns.

If you need eyeglasses to see, wear them. If you don't like the way they look on you, get contacts. There are few things more annoying than an actor who is squinting at a script or a cue card because he is too vain to wear glasses. You might want to invest in a couple of pairs of ''prop'' glasses. What you do is have them made with plain glass, preferably the non-glare type. An attractive pair of glasses can throw you immediately into a more businesslike or studious type range. And, of course, never, ever wear darkly tinted glasses to an audition unless they are asked for.

Regarding your weight: a double standard exists. Men gain weight, and they just get more ''character''; women gain weight, and they are chubby. Women in the twenty-to-forty age range need to be the most cautious about weight gain. In terms of type, it is better to be slim or outright fat. That chunky look can cost you work. For my money, the best bet is to let your health dictate your weight anyway.

3

Casting Directors

Casting directors work for producers. Some of them free-lance and are available to any producer who wants to hire them, and others have full-time staff positions with ad agencies, television networks, movie studios, or production houses. Some operate out of their own plush offices, others out of their apartments; some specialize in casting movies or stage, others in commercials or TV shows; some are men, and some are women. Whatever their personal situation, their function is always the same: the casting director's primary job is to go out into the world and find actors to audition for the director and producers. Once the director and producers have decided which actors they want to hire, the casting director is the one who negotiates money, schedules, and billing with the actors and/or their agents.

HOW CASTING DIRECTORS WORK

As far as producers are concerned, a casting director can find actors wherever and however he pleases, but the most common way by far is through franchised talent agents. In a city like Los Angeles, there are something like two hundred agents who are continually pursuing the casting directors, trying to get their clients in on the auditions. The numbers may be smaller in Detroit, San Francisco or Dallas, but the procedures are exactly the same. Casting directors usually talk to agents when they want actors.

The very term "casting director" is something of a buzzword to people in the entertainment industry, conjuring up all kinds of associative images and emotions. To new actors, casting directors can be a great frustration because it might be hard to meet them; to actors who have been around the track a couple of times, the complaint is that casting directors see them in too narrow a type range. To the talent agent, a casting director may be Mr. Wonderful or a pain in the rear, but if you want to get your clients in to see him, you have to make nice. To a producer, a casting director is the only thing protecting him from that tidal wave of actors out there.

At its finest, casting is more of an art than a craft. An intuitive, insightful, empathetic casting director is worth more than his weight in gold to both the producers and the actors. At its most mundane, it is little more than a traffic-cop function and demands respect from few. Casting directors have no union (though they do have a society now), and there is no school that teaches the skill. Usually they learn through an informal apprenticeship. Their backgrounds are as varied as the listings in the Yellow Pages. I've seen secretaries, flight attendants, photographers, industry wives, and talent agents become casting directors, but I suspect the most common denominator is that many were aspiring actors at one time. More than a few have stuck a toe in the water to see about acting, jerked it out immediately, and instead gone into casting.

The relationship between actors and casting directors is fascinating, because no matter how much personal chemistry there might be, an actor can never get it out of his head that this is a person who can broker a job, and the casting director can never forget that he is dealing with an actor who badly wants to work. Most of the time, everybody deals with one another in a professional manner, and that is what you should expect if you are a newcomer. Tales of "casting couches'' and such are overblown. As in any business, how-ever, standards can break down from time to time, and, when they do, the result can be embarrassment, awkward-ness, or outright injury. I really don't think it is necessary for new people to wear a suit of armor when approaching cast-ing directors, but if you find yourself in a situation that feels uncomfortable, move carefully. You absolutely, positively do not have to compromise yourself in any way to further your acting career, especially sexually or financially.

At an audition, the casting director is the actor's ally. He wants you to do a good job, wants you to get cast. If you look good, he looks good. Remember, he is bringing you into the audition room to meet his boss, the producer. Therefore, pay close attention to little signals he might send, helpful hints he might give you while escorting you into a reading. I can't count the jobs I have gotten because the casting director whispered in my ear that ''they're looking for something really low-key and natural'' or ''they don't know what they want, be bold.'' He may work for the producer, but the casting director is your friend.

PRE-SCREEN INTERVIEWS WITH CASTING DIRECTORS

If a casting director doesn't already know your work, it is understandable that he would want to pre-screen you before taking you to the director and producers. The way in which this is done varies a bit from medium to medium, however, so we have to look at each one separately.

Commercial pre-screens rarely involve a sit-down chat be-cause commercial auditions are typically videotaped. The casting director has the opportunity to get to know an actor during this first taping and has the option of erasing him from the tape before forwarding it to the ad agency.

TV and movie pre-screens involve a private conversation and a cold reading from ''sides'' (selected pages from a script). The casting director will look at your photo and resume and then ask you to read for him. If he likes the reading, he'll go ahead and schedule a time for you to come back and audition for the producers and director. If you are already an actor with some strong credits, a pre-screen will probably only involve "taking a meeting." Until you get to that point, bring your reading glasses.

Stage pre-screens usually include a private chat and an opportunity for you to present a couple of prepared monologues. For more about how to select and present monologue material, see "Auditioning for the Stage."

The biggest problem with pre-screen interviews is that they are frequently sandwiched into a casting director's busy day. Everybody is in a hurry. The telephone may be ringing, people may be going in and out of the casting director's office, and he may be distracted. Don't lose your cool if this happens. Hopefully, he will ask for privacy while meeting you, but if not, keep a sense of humor and go with the flow. If the casting director seems distracted during the actual reading, wait for him. The actor always has the power to set the pace in a scene. If "sides" are given to you cold, ask for a few minutes to look at them. Don't try to impress the casting director with what a quick study you are. Return to the outer office and analyze the script; mark it up if you want to. You need to have the advantage if you can gain it. Also, if you can incorporate what is going on in the office into your reading, do so. I once had a situation where I was reading a scene that called for a furious outburst. Just as I was getting to the outburst part, the phone started ringing. Clearly, the casting director didn't want to interrupt my reading, so she just let the thing ring. Finally, I stopped, looked right at her, and through clenched teeth ordered her to answer the phone— just as if it were part of the scene. She took the call while I sat there, still in the script situation. When she hung up, I picked up the scene right where I left off, using the interruption to further fuel the anger necessary for the scene. It worked: I wound up returning to read for the director and got the job.

HELPFUL HINTS FOR AUDITIONS OR PRE-SCREENS

These suggestions apply to any kind of audition or pre-screen you might get:

- Don't eat a heavy meal before auditioning. It will make you feel leaden, and the nerves may give you terrible indigestion.

- Don't drink alcohol before an audition thinking it will calm your nerves. It won't. All it will do is throw off your timing.

- Don't drink too much coffee or smoke too many cigarettes before an audition. They both will make you anxious.

- Get a good night's sleep before an audition.

- Carry a breath spray with you. Nervous energy causes all kinds of body and breath odors, and if you are working in a close space, you want to be ready.

- Don't wear clothing that shows perspiration stains if you are the kind of person who sweats when nervous. I also suggest you use a super-strong antiperspirant.

- It is a good idea to always be ready with a chatty story of some kind, an ice-breaker. Some people like to talk about their kids, or maybe you are planning a trip to China. I'm not talking about a monologue, just a subject that interests you that might involve a casting director or producer if the situation should arise. Some people, particularly those in the movie world, may purposely draw you into casual conversation to see your "real" personality, and sometimes these situations just happen by chance. I recall a time when preparation in this area really came in handy. I was auditioning for a Neil Simon movie, and Mr. Simon was in the room. While the director was looking at my resume, Mr. Simon asked me what I had been up to lately, and I mentioned a recent fishing trip. To my surprise, he liked fishing! So, before the reading even started, I had the chance to schmooze with Neil Simon for a few minutes. Couldn't hurt.

- Don't waste time in the waiting room by socializing with other actors. Stay focused on your work.

- Don't worry so much about what you think they are looking for. Show them how the role will be played if they cast you. Put your stamp on it.

PART TWO

AUDITIONING

4

Auditioning for TV Commercials

Commercials are where the money is. American companies spend $9 billion (that's billion with a "b") each year on them. Members of Screen Actors Guild earn upwards of $340 million annually from this source, accounting for 40 percent of total SAG income! In fact, 10 percent of the respondents to a 1983 SAG survey identified themselves as "commercial actors" instead of simply "actors" and evidently have little interest in appearing in anything else.

You don't need a Ph.D. to understand what is going on in commercials, and you don't have to be a graduate of the Royal Academy to act in them. That's why every Aunt Hilda and her niece wants to do them. When I am traveling around the country and people discover that I teach audition technique for commercials, I invariably find hopefuls lining up for an honest appraisal. "People tell me I have a good face for commercials," they will explain. "Do you think I ought to try it?" It's amazing, really. Sober, responsible adults, people who wouldn't dream of getting up on the stage and acting in a play, are ready to drop everything for the chance to be in a Pampers spot. I've had doctors, lawyers, dentists, and even the ambassador to Nepal in my classes, and every time another Clara Peller situation ("Where's the beef?") is publicized, there is all the more interest.

Let's settle it right off, then. Can a non-actor, a regular housewife or a retired cop, make it in commercials? Yep. Is it easy to do it? Not by a long shot. Commercials are not something you pursue on a lark. They require an investment of time, money and persistence, and the average performer only gets one commercial out of every forty auditions or so. A non-actor who wants to do commercials should reread the first paragraph of this chapter and really reflect on how much money SAG members earn from commercials. Those people are your competition. When you go to auditions, they will be sitting next to you, and it can be unnerving to realize the determination of the average professional actor.

The bright side for the non-actor is that commercials are getting shorter and are using less dialogue. Fully 25 percent of all spots on TV now are only fifteen seconds long, and the trend is bound to continue. When I did my first commercial (for Holiday Inns) in 1970, almost all spots were sixty seconds long with wall-to-wall dialogue. As ad costs have risen, spots have gotten shorter and are relying much more on mood music and quick-cut editing. In other words, if there is anything that professional actors have over non-professionals, it is the ability to use dialogue effectively, and there just isn't as much demand for that skill today as there used to be. It equalizes things a bit.

LIFE AS PORTRAYED IN COMMERCIALS

Consumer Reports magazine did a study of commercials once and discovered that only one in eighteen conveyed any useful information at all. The point of most spots is to reinforce the name of the product in a positive way, to make the viewer feel good about it. That's why they convey the sense of life that they do.

Can you imagine an entire town populated by the people you see in commercials? No serial killers there, eh? You also won't find overcrowded classrooms, burn centers, corrupt politicians, or dogs with no homes. It's an idyllic world, one in which everyone is happy, healthy (or at least jolly), doesn't need to be too concerned about world events, and is eager to get up in the morning and get at that bowl of cereal. Also, no one reads a lot of books. Let's take a closer look.

The Commercial Woman:

- likes to do housework. A dirty wall is just another opportunity.

- likes to trade little household secrets with girlfriends.

- spends a lot of time shopping.

- takes care of house and home even if she is holding down a full-time job. She's a kind of good-natured super woman.

- never gets depressed or sees a shrink.

- always has enough energy left at the end of the day to light those romantic candles.

The Commercial Man:

- brings home the bacon.

- knows next to nothing about household products. Send him to the store for a cleanser, and he will invariably bring home the less expensive Brand X.

- always makes enough money to afford a house with a nice big yard, usually big enough for a sit-down type mower.

- only displays intelligence when it comes to buying cars, insurance, camping equipment, beer, or computers.

- is an avid sports fan.

The Commercial Kid is always cute, scruffy, and precocious.

Because commercials portray such an innocent, conservative sense of life, and because women are normally seen as homemakers, sophisticated actresses can sometimes be offended by them. Women's rights have been the subject of long, difficult battles, and it can be frustrating to turn on your TV and see women whose primary interest seems to revolve around the search for a better toilet-bowl cleanser.

I mention this because I have encountered the problem so many times in my classes, and it is critical that it be overcome. If the ad agency executives suspect that you are harboring resentment about the way a woman is portrayed in a spot, they will pass on you. They really want to cast actors who are "team players," people who are wholeheartedly joining in the sales effort.

If this is a problem for you, try this perspective: a commercial is an acting job just the same as if you were acting in a TV show or a movie. Acting is acting. If you were hired to portray a commercial star in the next Jane Fonda movie, could you do it honestly? If you had to portray somebody who did not harbor resentment, could you? If you are a good actress, you could.

If you cannot, absolutely will not, get your head around this, then I think it would be a wise move not to get involved with commercials at all. The ad agency people will see right through you when they replay the tapes, and you will just be in for a lot of frustration. Life is too short to do things that you really don't want to do.

Commercials are the very last medium to reflect changes in mores and fashions. First, change shows up in the movies or on stage, then on television shows, and finally in commercials. They tend to reflect a view of society that is about ten years behind, and the emphasis is on maintaining the status quo. The last thing Madison Avenue wants to do is offend somebody with adventuresome commercials.

Just to give you an idea of how conservative they really are, consider the following taboos: you never see toilet paper next to the toilet in commercials. Ever notice? It can be rolling down the steps or getting squeezed in a market, but it never appears where it actually goes. Douche commercials never precisely mention what a douche is used for; you never see an actual picture of a tampon or feminine napkin; and you never see anybody actually take an aspirin or any other kind of pill.

But don't confuse conservative with stupid. The people who create and produce commercials know exactly what they are doing. Market research is their middle name and, if they are conservative in their approach, it is only because they know for certain that that is the best way to sell the product.

Recently, I saw a copy of *The Wall Street Journal* that contained an amazing article on the degree of market research done in advertising. It involved a study done by the McCann-Erickson advertising agency in which they tried to determine why the female consumer prefers spray-can roach killers to the "roach hotel" variety. According to the article, women will buy the spray even if they believe the "hotel" to be a superior product.

So what the agency did was get a group of women together and ask them to draw pictures of roaches—with their left hands. Since the right hemisphere of the brain is visual, symbolic, and emotional, and controls the left half of the body, drawing with the left hand taps into perceptions better. Then, after the pictures of roaches were drawn, the women were asked to write a little story explaining how they feel about the roaches. Well, surprise number one was that every single woman drew *male* roaches (I don't know, maybe they had on little ties or something), not female ones, so the ad agency figured all of this was symbolic of male/female relationships. Surprise number two was that, in the stories, it became clear that the women liked to watch the roaches squirm and die! A roach hotel might be a kinder, gentler, more effective product, but the user wouldn't get the kind of emotional satisfaction from it that she would from a spray.

The article went on to discuss female fears of male abandonment and such, but you get the idea. The point is, these folks are thorough when it comes to devising TV ads. Why, I have even done commercials for products that don't exist. The agency will make a sample product, the total output of which is on the commercial set. Then they'll do a spot and put it on the air in a test market like Oklahoma City, following up with phone calls to randomly-selected TV viewers. If

enough people answer the survey questions the right way,
then the manufacturer will go ahead and make some of the
product to sell. This is a cheaper procedure than gearing up
for manufacture first.

HOW COMMERCIALS ARE CAST

Once a casting director has his instructions from an ad
agency, he puts out calls to talent agents who suggest actors.
Audition times are scheduled, and actors show up at the
casting studio where their auditions are put on videotape.
Usually, only the actor and casting director are present at this
first audition. After that, the tape is reviewed by the ad
agency creative team, the director, and the client (the people
who make the product); they whittle the list of original actors
down to a handful who are asked to come to a ''callback.'' At
the callback, the actors repeat what they did at the first
audition, again being videotaped. The difference is that this
time, the actual director is there to give adjustments.

Casting decisions are made from this callback audition
except on the rare occasion when yet another callback is
scheduled. The commercial is shot within a week, as a rule.

Regarding what to wear to a commercial audition: both
men and women should stick with pastels, muted colors,
earth tones. Stay away from busy patterns, paisleys, that
kind of thing. Also, avoid shirts or sweaters that are solid
red, white, or black. The reason for this is that those colors
draw attention from your face.

Women should have in their wardrobes a number of
sweater/shirt combinations and some skirts. Slacks are fine if
they aren't too tight. A business suit is a necessity, particularly if you are thirty or older. Sportswear is a definite
yes. At minimum, you should have the type of sportswear
that you might put on to go bike-riding or jogging. Jeans can
be okay at times, but be careful. I would advise against them
unless you know for certain they are appropriate.

Men should also have some sweater/shirt combos and
some slacks. Chinos are great. Plaids or pastels are good.
A blue blazer and slacks are a wonderfully flexible outfit. A

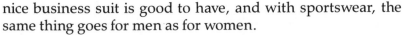
nice business suit is good to have, and with sportswear, the same thing goes for men as for women.

Everybody should avoid dangling jewelry, things that catch the light.

WORKING WITH VIDEOTAPE

Virtually all commercial auditions are recorded on videotape, a factor that distinguishes them immediately from the ''live'' auditions held for TV shows, movies, and stage. Videotape didn't appear until about 1970 but, in just a few years, it has revolutionized the world of commercials.

> FACT: Videotape makes it possible for the ad agency to tap into a national talent pool. Actors in San Francisco and Orlando now routinely audition for commercials that originate in New York or L.A.

> FACT: Videotape has created a whole new job category, that of the independent casting director. There needs to be some way to technically reach the talent pools in the cities of America, and the free-lance casting director is part of the equation.

> FACT: Videotape positively must be mastered as a medium by anyone who seriously wants to act in commercials. You may be a wonderful stage actor, but you can still get befuddled by videotape cameras.

> FACT: Videotape puts a barrier between actors and their potential employers. Auditioning on tape is quite a different situation than being able to walk in and shake hands with the nice people.

I have seen many fine actors turn to mush in front of a videotape camera. It's not like working in a movie, where you rarely look directly into the lens of the camera. Suddenly, you are expected to not only look into the lens, but to relate to it, all the while maintaining a chipper and energetic demeanor. Some people behave as though they have met their first Martian and, basically, would rather be in Philadelphia.

The camera tells the truth, nothing more and nothing less. It doesn't amplify things, and it doesn't make you look different than you do in life. Maybe it is because people sense this that they want to withdraw from the scrutiny. It is embarrassing to have the truth about you shown on a TV screen! And, of course, as soon as you begin to withdraw, that becomes the reality that the camera sees, and when the ad agency people replay the tape later, they see an actor who doesn't want to be there. Why hire him?

Good news: if the videotape camera is the dragon of your worst nightmares, you'll be happy to learn that the dragon can definitely be tamed. It is possible to come across on camera as warm and personable. How? By personalizing the camera. That means you have to develop the craft of being able to talk to a camera as if it might talk back to you.

New people as well as experienced actors frequently have the mistaken notion that, when you talk into the lens of the camera, you should be performing a commercial for the camera to take a picture of. They equate it roughly to the transaction that took place when Mom used to point the Brownie and instruct them to ''say cheese.'' This is not that. Talking into a videotape camera at a commercial audition is a one-of-a-kind thing. You are not performing for the camera, and you are not talking to ''America.'' What you are doing is trying to make it seem like you are talking to each *individual* person who is watching the replay or the commercial, and the way you do that is to pretend that the camera is one person.

Children have no trouble at all with this concept. In fact, they love it. I taught a group of kids once, and was fascinated by the ways they would play with the camera. ''Pretend the camera is Mom,'' I would tell them. ''Okay!'' they would respond, ''where's Dad?'' For them, it was just a game. Adults have learned to be inhibited, though, have learned what it means to be embarrassed. They are afraid they will look silly if they talk to a camera as if it is a person who might talk back. ''I wouldn't dance with a mop in the middle of Hollywood Boulevard, and I won't talk to a camera as if it is a person who might talk back,'' they seem to say.

I'm going to ask you to do something that you may never have done before, and I think it will help you understand the kind of transaction that is necessary between you and the videotape camera.

Look around the room you are sitting in right at this moment until you find something small and inanimate that you can relate to. That light switch over by the door will do just fine. Now, tell the light switch hello. Go ahead, do it. Don't worry about being silly. Just look right at the light switch, smile, and say "Hello!" Did it react to you? It did? Well, then you need to see a doctor. Light switches don't react, and wishing won't make it so. But—are you ready?—you can *pretend* that it did! You can pretend that, when you said hello, the light switch grinned, flipped its little toggle, and said "Hiya!" right back. Now, you in turn react to the light switch's greeting. If you really want to test the relationship you have with your new friend, go ahead and tell him about the wonderful time you had on your last vacation. Pretend that he is loving the story, is eager to hear more. Build up to the most exciting part, the moment when you met Mr. or Ms. Right walking on the beach. You are happy, the light switch is happy, everybody is happy! Okay, the exercise is complete. If the light switch had been a videotape camera at an audition, you would have been relating correctly. You see? It isn't the same thing as talking *at* the light switch; you have to talk *with* it, to communicate with it.

Words express a thought, right? You can also express a thought with a kiss or a kick in the shin or a bear hug. The important thing is that expressing a thought implies the presence of another person—you need somebody to express *to*. That other person at a commercial audition is frequently the camera. When you begin talking to another person, you check his reaction to what you are saying so that you can tell how to proceed. That is why the punch line is at the end of the joke rather than at the beginning. You start telling the joke and, watching the person to be sure he is following you, you build up to the punch line. If you were to be talking to a person and saw a look of non-comprehension, you'd have to drop back and rephrase what you just said before you could move forward.

I realize it is a little awkward to dissect communication in this fashion, but it is the easiest way to learn how to relate to an inanimate object like a camera. In life, we don't usually inspect the way we communicate on a frame-by-frame basis, but it can be a useful exercise in this context.

Are there any exceptions? The only one I can think of is something comedic. I have seen a few commercials where the actors are purposely doing a parody of someone who does not relate to the camera, someone like a game show host or a newscaster. TV news people are frequently too busy reading the teleprompter to relate to the camera. And, of course, game-show hosts are notorious for slickness and non-involvement. They paste on a big plastic smile, look right into the camera, and talk to A-M-E-R-I-C-A! But, as I say, the exceptions are few. You'll be safe if you presume that you should always relate with the camera unless a specific situation demands otherwise.

Now, in commercials that involve couples or groups of people acting out situations, the camera becomes an audience to the scene, and the actors should not look at it. The thing to remember is that if you look directly into the lens of the camera, it breaks the "fourth wall." When you do it, you are bringing the person who is watching the TV right into the scene with you, just the same as if you turned around on stage and addressed the fellow in the front row.

For example, if you are reading for a spot in which a husband and wife are in the bathroom discussing deodorants, you certainly wouldn't want to address the camera. If you did, you would bring a third person into the bathroom with you. The same thing would be true for a romantic spot on a deserted Hawaiian beach. There isn't anybody else out there, and if you talk to the camera, you break the illusion.

But, you can do an "aside" just the way you would in the theater. In fact, it can be extremely effective. Suppose the situation involved a bunch of people sitting quietly in a library reading room. Suddenly, this fellow starts munching on Fritos. Crunch! The script may only indicate that the guy next to him is supposed to be surprised, that he should jump and be startled. It would be absolutely wonderful to do a slow "take" to camera in such a case. It would be okay because we are in a place where there are a lot of people, and theoretically, the viewer at home is one of them. Get it?

And then, of course, there is always the situation where it is written in the script itself that everybody on camera relates to the camera. There are lots of spots like this. Just remember that the camera is *one* person.

The main challenge when working with other people on camera is to make sure you are seen in as many planes as possible. If life, you might stand toe-to-toe when talking to your friend, but if you do that on camera, you'll only be seen in profile. Instead, you have to "cheat" out. Instead of toe-to-toe, stand shoulder-to-shoulder at a slight angle to the camera.

Having said all of this, I guarantee that you will encounter situations where the casting director will tell you point blank that he wants you to look into the camera on a particular line, and you will know fully well that it is inappropriate to do it. I would rather see you get the job and get paid than be right, so don't snicker and don't argue with him. Let him do his job. He may have his own reasons for wanting you to look into the camera. Maybe the folks at the ad agency asked for it.

You have to know what is correct technique, how perspective and point of view work. That way, if you run into an exception, you'll treat it as just that, and you'll return to a firm base with the next audition.

"RESULT" DIRECTION

At commercial auditions, you are going to get a kind of direction that you rarely get at auditions for stage, movies, or television shows—"result" direction. What that means is that the casting director is going to tell you the precise "result" he wants to see in your audition. For example, he'll say: "Make it animated," "Warm it up, lots of eyes," "Play it macho," "Be broad, have fun with it," "They're looking for big facial reactions on this one."

An experienced theatrical director will usually give an actor "situational" direction, and, in fact, it is a sign of a weak director to resort to asking for "results." A good director will set up the situation for you, perhaps suggest an objective, and then let you play it as you will. If he doesn't like it, he will change the objective or some circumstance in order to alter your performance. For example, a seasoned director might set up a situation this way: ''You've just arrived at your home and discover the front door is ajar. You push it open and enter only to discover the furniture in disarray. Your spouse is nowhere to be seen, and the place is quiet. Suddenly, you hear an object fall on the floor upstairs. Go and see what it is.'' Result direction for the same situation would be: ''You've just arrived home and discover the front door is ajar. Tense up as you slowly push the door open to discover the furniture in disarray. Big shocked expression on your face. Suddenly, you hear an object fall on the floor upstairs. Freeze in your steps. Look to your left and right. Then quietly go see what the noise was. You should be very fearful and anxious.''

The reason that casting directors for commercials so frequently give this kind of direction is that they take their instructions from ad agency people, and, as we have already discussed, these people are not in the entertainment business at all. The ad agency's producer may tell the casting director that he is looking for several actors who are ''broadly animated,'' for example, and the casting director will carry that right into the audition. Rather than direct situationally, he'll say, ''Lot's of animation on this . . . big faces, the bigger the better . . . very broad . . . have fun with it.''

Lesson number one in any basic acting class is that you cannot act a ''result.'' It is impossible to act ''animation,'' and it is impossible to act ''broad.'' If you try to do it, you'll only succeed in making faces for no reason at all; your acting will be unmotivated. The fact is that acting means *doing* something. You have to pursue objectives, play specific actions.

Clearly, I can't teach someone to act in a few paragraphs. If this concept of ''results'' versus ''actions'' is alien to you, I strongly suggest you get yourself into a good acting workshop. Understanding this type of thing is precisely what separates the non-actor from the professional, and it is the primary reason the bulk of the jobs go to the pros. If you don't know how to convert ''result'' direction to something active, you'll be almost totally dependent on your physical type and winning sense of life to get you cast in commercials. That may do the trick a small percentage of the time, but you'll be operating at a decided disadvantage.

For now, here are a couple of sample ''result'' directions and suggested responses to them.

I'm at an audition for Wendy's, and the situation calls for me to eat a burger and say to the camera, ''Now, that's a good burger!'' I do it once, and the casting director says, ''Do it again. Much more energy. Much broader.'' I do a second take, and this time pretend that I've been on the desert for the past week with no food to eat. I'm famished. I dig into the burger with all my heart, and ''Now, that's a good burger!'' comes out with twice the gusto as before. I didn't try to play it more broadly or with more energy. What I did was raise the stakes situationally. Get it?

I'm at an audition for an antiperspirant product, straight spokesman material. I give it my best shot, and the casting director says I should ''warm it up, more one-to-one.'' I do a second take, this time pretending that I am talking to a woman instead of a man. The net result is a warmer reading.

The trick is to listen to what the casting director tells you, and then to translate that into something that is playable. That's your job, it's what they pay you for. A casting director really isn't there to teach you how to act, and the concept of playing an action will ideally be second nature to you.

PREPARING FOR THE AUDITION

When you arrive at the casting studio, fill out the SAG sign-in sheet on the table (yes, even if you're not in SAG, fill it out), pick up a copy of the script from the stack next to the sign-in sheet, and glance around to see if there is a storyboard taped to the wall.

A storyboard is a cartoon depiction of the commercial. It looks like a black and white version of the Sunday comics, with each panel representing a different shot of the commercial. Not every commercial has a storyboard at the audition, and you don't absolutely have to have one, but they can be helpful. Commercial copy sometimes appears oblique unless you know what the visuals will be.

You'll have five to fifty minutes before you'll be called into the audition room. If they keep you longer than an hour, the casting director gets fined by SAG, so these things tend to move along. Expect to spend about fifteen minutes on average.

There are various kinds of commercials you are likely to encounter. For a spot with copy, on camera alone (very common), you stand all by yourself and talk directly to the camera. A spot with copy, on camera with a group might encompass anything from a football stadium full of people to a husband and wife in the bathroom. For a spot with no copy, on camera alone or with a group (also very common), you will usually be doing an improvisational audition (See ''Improvisational Auditions'').

The first thing to do is to read the spot carefully. Be sure you can pronounce everything and that you understand every single sentence and nuance. If in doubt, ask the casting director during one of his trips to the waiting room. Next, categorize the commercial in terms of style. Is it a pie-in-the-face slapstick kind of thing? Is it a warm puppy dog? Slice-of-life? Straight spokes? Who is the target audience? Women? Teens? This information will help you when trying to figure out who you might be talking to when you look into the camera. What advertising claims are being made about the product? What are they saying is special about it? Remember, advertising is about getting people to buy product A instead of product B on the premise that they'll buy something from this product category anyway. Most commercials contain an implied comparison.

Now you're ready to start looking at the copy from a first-person perspective. The thought process goes: ''Okay, what am I (not what is the character) doing in this spot?'' Own it. Ask yourself these questions:

Where am I? In other words, what is the location of the commercial? Does it take place in a parking lot? In a bedroom? At a soccer game?

Who am I talking to? What is my relationship with him or her? If you are talking to the camera, who is it? You can't talk to "America," remember. With most copy, there may be no clue at all, so you'll have to create a relationship.

If you are on camera with other people, who are they? Do you know them, or are they strangers? Relationship is everything, and the more specific you are about it, the better. A husband/wife relationship calls for intimacy of the fanny-slapping variety right from the start, for instance. Why am I telling my girlfriend about this detergent? Why am I buying this new TV set? Why are we at the restaurant? Is it our anniversary or just a casual date? Again, you may well have to impose choices of this sort, because many commercials don't even give a clue.

If there is no dialogue, no copy, then what are my actions? Why am I doing what I'm doing? Motivate, motivate, motivate!

All right, you've answered all of the questions. Now you can start rehearsing. I personally think the best way is to speak the words out loud if there are any. Go find a light switch to talk to, or go out in the parking lot and chat with a car. Do anything except sit there and meditate on it. If you have a two-person spot, you might want to run over it with the other actor, but the problem is that you can't be sure who that is. The casting director may very well have you matched up on a list he is carrying around with him, so you can't presume that you will be reading with the next person on the sign-in sheet. Therefore, you may not be able to rehearse with the other actor. Anyway, some actors don't like to rehearse with others in waiting rooms. They like to save all of the surprises and juice for the camera. If you know for sure who will be reading with you, go ahead and ask if he wants to rehearse. If he demurs, don't be offended.

When rehearsing, stay away from mirrors! This is another of those items that is the subject of much bad advice. I've heard many supposedly knowledgeable individuals tell aspiring actors that they should rehearse in front of mirrors, and it is merely an indication that the advice-giver really doesn't understand what actors do. The fact is, you can't be on the stage and in the audience simultaneously, right? If you're on the stage and you want to be in the audience, you have to walk down those little steps to get there. Well, when you rehearse in front of a mirror, you are trying to force an impossible issue; you're trying to be both actor and audience at the same time. You're acting and watching yourself to see how you're doing.

You can always tell which actors have been rehearsing in front of mirrors because, when they get into the audition room, they have terminal cases of the "cutes." They stand in the bathroom and work out where to wink and smile and giggle, and then they come into the audition room and try to recreate what they did in the bathroom! That's not acting, that's mimicry. And, anyway, if you try to do it, you'll only hurt yourself as an actor. Keep the process conceptual: where am I? Who am I talking to? Why am I telling him this?

MEMORIZING AND CUE CARDS

Anybody who has ever done one-week stock knows that memorizing is a learned skill. After a summer spent rehearsing one play in the daytime, performing another one at night, and then changing plays every week, you get to the point where you go to breakfast and walk away having memorized the menu! You train yourself to accomplish a kind of surface-level memorization, and as soon as the summer is over, all of it vanishes from your brain.

At commercial auditions, you don't have to memorize the copy unless you want to. They will have a nice big piece of posterboard right next to the camera with the words printed on it in magic marker. SAG has a rule about this, and the casting director can actually face a fine if a cue card is not in use for a commercial that has copy. All you have to do is relate to the camera; when you forget what comes next, glance over at the cue card, get the words, and bring them back to camera.

As easy a process as this seems, I see actors get thrown by cue cards all of the time. Because the words are right there in their faces, they feel compelled not to make a single mistake.

Rather than concentrate on the logic of the piece, they worry about the words. They want to stare at the card, but fear that it will look odd on camera if they do. The cue card therefore becomes a distraction rather than an aid.

The easiest thing to do is simply memorize the copy and be done with it. You'll get a small competitive edge if you do. If you are skittish about it, however, you'll only cripple your audition by pressuring yourself to memorize. You may have the copy firmly in your head in the waiting room and then, under pressure of the actual audition, it evaporates; you wind up standing there looking at the camera while scanning an internal script. On replay, you can see a fixed look in the eyes rather than the warmth of communication. It comes across as a variation of self-doubt.

If you want to learn to memorize quickly, get in the practice of finding the logic of the copy right away. When you pick up the script in the waiting room, resist the temptation to start memorizing right away. If you get the logic first, you'll find the words in the copy are the only ones that will make sense. That way, even if you get something wrong, you'll get right back on track because you understand the points you need to make. This kind of memorization isn't like learning the books of the Bible or a grocery list. There is a flow to it.

If you are really bothered by the idea, however, try this compromise: commit the first thought, whether it be one, two or three lines, to memory. That way, after you slate your name and "action" is called, you won't begin your audition by looking at a card instead of the camera. You'll involve the viewer immediately. Then refer to the card in the middle of the spot, even if you have to read that entire section. At the end, have the last thought in your memory for a strong finish.

You need not make yourself crazy over each comma and period in the copy. If you mess up a little, nobody will hold it against you. Just don't rewrite the spot. The ad agency execs know that auditions are rough, that you only have a few minutes to spend with the commercial before reading, and they figure you will get it memorized correctly by the time the spot is shot. This isn't an invitation to engage in wholesale paraphrasing, only permission to be human.

One more thing: when you are standing in front of the camera, it can seem like you are shifting your gaze from New York to Paris when you go back and forth between the camera and cue card. It may seem like that at the time, but it doesn't look that way on replay, so don't worry about it.

THE AUDITIONING PROCESS

You'll usually find yourself alone in there with the casting director, sometimes with a camera operator. There will be some simple but bright lighting, and a 3/4-inch videotape set-up (which is the industry standard).

The casting director will guide you to your "mark" and tell you what he wants you to do in the audition. If it involves any blocking, this is where that will be made clear. This is also the time to ask any questions you have about the spot.

Take the time to read the cue card even if you are confident that you have memorized the copy. Because the lines on the cue card are written in magic marker, there are fewer words per line than with typewritten script; if you have to refer to it during the reading, you don't want to be searching around for your place. Also, the announcer's lines will not be on the card, because those lines are not spoken aloud in the audition. The exception would be if the actor on camera has to react to an off-camera speaker, in which case the casting director will read them, but they are almost always omitted. When you read the card, move your lips so the casting director will know when you're through. He is frequently a bit impatient to get on with it because there is a roomful of actors out there. Still, you must take the time to read the card.

If your reading involves a "now and later" situation, the casting director will usually stop the camera to allow for a passage of time. For instance, the "now" part may involve two girls talking about how awful their hair looks, and the "later" part takes place after the hero product has been used.

The casting director may want you to rehearse once before turning on the tape but, if he knows your work, he might just "tape the rehearsal." Personally, I don't like to rehearse these things unless there is a lot of complicated physical business like pouring coffee and holding up products.

When you're ready, the tape machine is turned on and the casting director asks you to "slate your name," or look into the lens and say who you are. Treat it like a warm handshake, an introduction, not like chalk on a blackboard. And for God's sake, pronounce your name clearly! It is a terrible thing to witness how mushy-mouthed some people get with their own names.

Then you'll get one or two takes, and that will be that. The casting director thanks you, you return to the waiting room, and sign out.

HANDLING PRODUCTS AND EATING FOOD

The only thing to remember about handling a product is not to wave it around while you are talking and to drop it away when you don't want to show it anymore. If you can, keep the product close to your face and try to position it so the camera can see the product name. Rather than hoisting up the product à la the Statue of Liberty, track the camera's "eyes" to make sure it is seeing what you are trying to display. The camera is a person, remember? Well, when you show somebody something, you track their eyes to make sure they saw it. This kind of nuance is what really gives an audition color and credibility.

If you are auditioning for a fast-food spot, you may well have to eat something. Hopefully, it will be something real, but if it isn't, be prepared to pretend to eat. This is a skill you *can* work on in front of a mirror. In fact, I spend time in my workshops doing nothing except working with actors on how to eat imaginary food. If they have crackers or something, which is often the case, just remember this: you are doing an audition for a food product, so it would help if you eat with gusto. Let the client think that, if it comes down to a choice between eating his wonderful product and talking, eating will almost win out. Let the food delight you.

IMPROVISATIONAL AUDITIONS

There are two basic kinds of improvisational auditions, *situational* and *sense-of-life*. A situational improv audition involves a set-up of some kind, and the actor is expected to actually do something. The sense-of-life audition involves nothing more than standing in front of the camera, giving a nice name slate, perhaps chatting with the casting director while the tape is rolling, and that's it. If you get either of those kinds, you can be sure that physical type is the primary consideration, so all you can do is be nice and not feel bad if you don't get cast.

Situational improv auditions need a bit of discussion. I went to one recently that was fairly typical, so I'll use that as an example. It was a spot for one of those stores that provides anything and everything for the do-it-yourself handyman, and the spot was divided into three parts. It began with Our Hero (me) shopping and then trying to go through check-out with all the boxes; then Our Hero and the wife are industriously hammering and painting a room; finally, they enjoy a moment of closeness as they survey their handiwork. Music up, fade out.

The casting director was shooting the audition in three set-ups, cutting between each. All he wanted to see on the first part was a shopper buying more stuff than he could rightly carry. On "action," I elected to actually bobble the boxes, dropping one and trying to pick it up while laughing at my awkwardness. Finally succeeding, I walked out of frame as we cut. The next section called for building something with the wife. The casting director said, "Okay, you two are busy. Ed, you are hammering and Claudia, you're painting. You are both into the task." Mind you, he never said what we were building, but I didn't really expect him to. In my mind, it was a nursery for the new baby. That choice gave me a nice positive initiative to build and a reason to smile meaningfully at Claudia. I don't know what she was playing, but she smiled back. The last part involved us contentedly surveying what we had built. Rather than stand there like a rock, I chose to point out the place in the wall above the camera where I nailed up my secret creation.

Now, I've outlined my personal choices to give you an idea of how much latitude you have in an improv audition. With no dialogue to guide you, and minimal situational direction, you need to fill in a lot of blanks.

Another example: a spot for a hamburger chain. It calls for Our Hero to arrive at the outlet, to stand in line, and then to place his order with an elderly counterman. Hero is surprised to see on oldster back there instead of the usual teenager. Cut. Then, in the second part, Hero happily eats his burger as we watch the oldster industriously serving more customers in the background. Music up.

My choice for the first part was, number one, to arrive hungry, and number two, for this to be my very favorite place to eat. I made sure I was in a really excellent mood, pretending that I just that morning landed a part in a movie. Suddenly, there was the oldster. Why. . . . I *know* that guy! He lives right down my block! I laughed and bantered with him. Then, in the second part, I eat and reflect on what a nice discovery it was to see Old James working here at my favorite place.

Are you getting the idea? Motivate, motivate, motivate! Go for relationships. Do something. Give yourself actions to play even if the casting director doesn't provide them. In the fast-food spot, nobody said anything about me knowing the oldster. The direction was, ''You're surprised but pleased. Nice warm smile. . . . '' That is not an active direction, so I gave it substance.

It's okay to talk, shout, or make noise unless you are specifically told not to. A lot of actors make the mistake of turning into Marcel Marceau at these improv auditions. If they ask you to slate your name, you know they are recording sound, so go ahead and make noise if it is appropriate to the situation.

Remember that you are not being judged on your wit. In fact, there will be no dialogue at all in the final script. It's okay if your words are corny or even strange.

Find ways to animate your body during the audition. It looks much more interesting than simply standing there.

Try to imagine what the music track for the spot will be, and match your audition dynamic to it. They are going to cast people to match their music.

For the *sense-of-life* audition, you slate your name and chat with the casting director. Some actors get hives over this and hate to be scrutinized in this way. Remember, the only reason they are chatting with you is to have a reason to keep the camera on for a moment. Since the final spot obviously doesn't involve a situation that requires audition, they are focusing on type, so they just want to look at you. It's not a test, so relax. Nothing is expected of you.

It's not unusual to have the casting director ask you "What have you been up to lately?" or "Tell us about yourself"— open-ended questions that could be answered in any number of ways. Keep your responses brief and bright. If you can, try to be theatrically relevant. Tell him you've been auditioning a lot lately (even if it's not true), or mention the play you're rehearsing. If you have zero theatrical activity to talk about, then tell him about your last vacation or how you've been training your dog. The important thing is not to drone on and look defensive. The questions do not have right and wrong answers, and the only reason he asked them was to see you on camera for a minute or so. It is not an invitation to go into a ramble about how you were born poor and found your way to the big city.

As with a situational improv, try to animate yourself physically if at all possible. Try to imagine how the audition might look if they played it back with the sound off. Would you simply be there talking, never changing your expression or stance?

A special note to actors who live in cities other than New York, Hollywood, or Chicago: I realize that you have a day job and may not get as much theatrical activity as you want yet. Still, if asked to talk about yourself, keep in mind that this casting session might be going on in several cities at once, and your competition might be full-time actors. Therefore, avoid approaches like "Well, I've been working at the Bank of America for twelve years in the accounting department, but I'm not very happy, so I hope to get into acting" or "Now that I've been laid off by the phone company, I was thinking that commercials might be a good thing to do." If you don't have anything else to talk about, mention acting classes you are taking. And, again, be happy about it!

THE CALLBACK AUDITION

If you are called back, you will be going through the same audition a second time, now being directed by the actual director, probably in the presence of the ad agency team and the client.

Casting decisions at this point are highly subjective, a game of mix and match, of balancing type and personal chemistry. Physical characteristics such as family resemblance, hair color, and height take on great significance, and all of the actors there can technically do the spot or they wouldn't have been called back.

The director may give you direction that is radically different from that you had in your initial audition. If so, just go with whatever he says. Remember, he is showing off a bit for his boss, the ad agency producer, and he wants to put his scent on you. Try to make him look good.

Wear the same clothes you wore to the first audition. It's hard to know precisely what they are responding to in you, but it's best for them to see the same package that was on the tape walk in the room.

When you enter the room, there will be all of these people just kind of sitting around awkwardly. They may laugh nervously or outright ignore you. Try to make eye contact if you can, put them at ease. Those are the ad agency people and client, and they won't relax until later when they review the tape again.

If they start a mix-and-match process with you and the other actors in the waiting room, you can be certain it is all a matter of chemistry and complimentary types. Your talent isn't on the line, so relax. Whenever they team you up with another new partner, bend your performance to accommodate whatever he is doing.Try not to freeze your performance even if you have to go in and out of the room ten times.

The single biggest mistake actors make at callback is they figure they should recreate whatever they did at the first audition. Forget it. You can't do it. That performance is history. Even if the director says, ''We like what you did, just do that again,'' you can't do it. Play in the present moment.

Make it fresh. Anyway, if you worry about trying to recreate what you did before, you'll just make yourself nervous.

HELPFUL HINTS

After many years of teaching audition technique, I have seen certain problem areas arise again and again. This list isn't meant to be all-inclusive, but it will point you in the right direction. Read it before your next commercial audition.

- Your audition begins the moment you enter the room, not the moment the camera is turned on. Get yourself into gear early.

- Deal with mistakes with humor. Never apologize for a flubbed take.

- It is not the actor's job to sell the product. That job belongs to the ad agency. What you want to do is convey your delight at having discovered the product. Share that discovery with the camera.

- Husband/wife relationships are frequently played as mother/son relationships in commercials, especially if you are selling household products.

- Mentally bring the camera to you when you look at it, rather than "chase" it. In the first place, it makes you appear more confident, and in the second place, the camera operator has probably zoomed in a bit. Even though the camera may be twelve feet away from you in reality, it will look like five or six on replay.

- Never try to play your type. This is a particular problem for beautiful, sexy, and handsome folks. The reasoning goes: "I'm here for a sexy spot, so I am supposed to behave in a sexy manner." No. Let your type take care of that. You can't act handsome or sexy anyway.

- Pretend advertising claims are true. I love this one and use it all the time. As consumers, we are as cynical as everybody else and realize that commercial claims are frequently so much hot air. But what if they were true? Wouldn't they be worth talking about with enthusiasm? Suppose this new brand of pantyhose really was both durable and sheer? Suppose it were true instead of advertising blabber, wouldn't it be swell? Pretend it is true, and act accordingly.

- Pretend you personally invented the product and/or the product demonstration. It will give you more of a stake.

- The videotape camera can be your friend or your enemy. If it is your friend, you'll be glad to see it at each audition. You'll have an ally in the room.

- A sigh is almost always a sign of personal pain and is practically never appropriate in commercials. Usually, actors sigh in auditions because they are nervous and in great discomfort. Sighing only highlights it, so don't.

- Commercials frequently involve dancing raisins, talking pats of butter, and voices that come out of the sky. In life, such occurrences would cause you to run screaming from the house; in commercials, all of the little creatures are your buddies! Make friends with them. Let them delight you.

- When you are on camera alone, remember that you are usually bringing up the subject. The camera didn't ask. Speak with initiative, with intent to make a point.

- When working with another actor on camera, stand closer than you would in real life. Nobody likes strangers right up in their face, but you won't look too close on replay.

- Don't be afraid to physically touch another actor on camera.

- Always be ready to reverse roles.

- Never be skeptical about the advertising claims of the hero product. Be inquisitive or studious, but never negative.

- If the spot is for a food product, you can't go wrong by nibbling on it.

- Never direct the other actor, even if his performance is awful. Let the casting director do it.

- Remember, life was going on before the first line of copy, and it continues after the last line of copy. Don't end an audition with a "freeze frame."

- It's okay to add a "button," a short ad lib, at the end of a spot if the situation merits it. If the husband's last line in a spot was, "Honey, you're the best wife in the world," it would be a good button to say "Yeah, I know" or "And you're the best husband." The ad agency doesn't mind this at all, and if they do, they'll tell you.

- If you are auditioning for a "spokesperson" role, say for a bank or an insurance company, you can still be warm and personal when you relate to the camera. Institutions of that sort are viewed with suspicion by large segments of the population, and they are looking for actors who will create an image of accessibility. Let your business suit define you as corporate. Keep your performance down to earth. Don't be afraid to use humor, even with the driest copy.

5

Auditioning for Voice Work

"Voice work" is actually a convenient umbrella term that covers a garden full of different jobs. Even a partial list of the possibilities is impressive:

- Radio commercials
- Off-camera voices for TV commercials
- Slide/film narration
- Cartoon voices
- Trailers for movies
- Promos for TV shows
- Narration for corporate films
- Recordings of novels and other books
- Walla (crowd voices and such in films and TV)

And we haven't even mentioned specialized looping jobs where the need is for "soundalike" voices, or the burgeoning field of Voice Mail, in which human voices are being linked to computers. Performers are needed for the ''976'' telephone services as well as some of the toll-free ''800'' calls. A San Francisco actress is the voice in Fords, telling drivers to buckle up, and also the voice for a talking cash register. There are elevator voices, computerized telephone solicitations, low-frequency radio broadcasts used to sell real estate and to tell you where to park at the airport, and the voices of the ghosts in the Haunted House at Disney World. In short, if you can think of it, there is a good chance a voice can be put in it, and that adds up to an awful lot of employment.

The lion's share of the jobs in this field go to a relatively small group of performers, some of whom are actors with excellent careers on stage and in front of the camera, and some who only do voice work. What they have in common is that they are solid pros. No dilettantes here, nobody slipping in because she's a cute physical type. These folks know their way around a recording studio, and so the producers tend to hire them again and again.

For one thing, recording studios are usually rented by the hour rather than the day, so a premium is put on people who are fast and flexible. For another, there are technical considerations. Working with a microphone is part art and part craft, and nobody really wants to take the time to teach you the craft while they are paying you to work. How close should your mouth be to the mike? How do you relate to other performers in dialogue situations without actually looking at them? What adjustments would you make if you wanted to sound intimate? Enthusiastic? If you wanted to give the impression of being indoors? Outdoors? If the engineer tells you that you are ''popping,'' what do you do to correct it?

And, of course, there's the matter of versatility. When someone is hired to do cartoon voices, for instance, one session fee covers two voices, and for an additional 10 percent, they can get a third voice tossed in. Why pay three performers to do three voices when you can hire one versatile performer for a third of the price? And some of these people have versatility plus. Not long ago, I took a voice-over workshop that was offered by one of the shining lights of the field, a woman accustomed to having animated series on the air as well as miscellaneous commercials. I sat there on a Saturday morning in the living room of her home on Mulholland Drive and watched as she created the voice of a munchkin. Then she created the munchkin's brother. Then she created the munchkin's sister. And mother. It was a display of talent that was at once dazzling and sobering, and helped explain why a small group gets most of the work. Why would a producer *not* work with a person who can do that?

You have to make a particular effort to orient yourself to the world of voices, preparing demo tapes and networking with the agents, casting directors, and producers who specialize in it. Your on-camera skills are only marginally useful when nobody can see your face, so you have to learn a whole other way of working. However, if you turn out to be talented, there is quite a pot at the end of this rainbow.

Auditions are held regularly for most voice jobs, so you'll be able to give it a shot if you want. One exception is the oddly-named field of Walla, in which performers record crowd noise for films and TV shows. Any time you see a scene in a bus station or cafeteria or rock concert, you can bet a Walla group had some input. The performers gather in a studio, watch the scenes on a movie screen, and simultaneously record the sound. This is in addition to occasional "dialogue replacement"—putting voices in the mouths of on-screen performers, usually because location sound recording was muddy or otherwise flawed. This has to be one of the more specialized activities in the entire world—the union rules governing it are a maze—but there are approximately 40 groups working in the field in Hollywood, where they can be in close proximity to the large studios. I recently spoke with Mickie McGowan, owner of Lip Shtick, one of the premier companies, responsible for Walla on such films as *Who Framed Roger Rabbit?* and *Terms of Endearment.* She explained that the demands of this work are so unique that open auditions aren't practical. Her preference is to work with actors who have experience in TV and movies and who have improvisation training; she finds them, or they find her, through networking, and her best advice to those who want to break in is to network extensively! Talk to other actors, seek out Walla groups and the people who run them, and make it your business to get a resume, photo, and voice tape (if you have one) to them. When you consider that the pay for one day of Walla on a TV show is $398, plus rerun residuals, it may be worth it.

HOW VOICE CASTING WORKS

Just as there are casting directors who specialize in on-camera commercials, there are those who do nothing but cast voices. Instead of a studio with a videotape camera and lights, they have one with a sound booth in it. And just as there are talent agents who represent on-camera performers, there are those who specialize in voices.

If an ad-agency producer has a radio commercial he wants to cast, he has several options. He can call agents and have them send performers to the ad agency to audition; he can hire an independent casting director, who will contact agents, having performers audition at the casting director's location; or, as is increasingly the preference, he can send the script directly to the agents, most of whom have their own in-agency recording booths and a FAX machines to receive the script. If the producer chooses this last method, then the agents will individually record their own clients and then send their tapes into the ad agency as their submissions. If he goes with a casting director, he'll just get one tape. Or, to confuse matters even further, he might employ a casting director *and* send scripts to some agents.

One way or another, the performers wind up in a record-ing booth somewhere. The layout is pretty much the same wherever you are. The booth is inevitably about as big as a walk-in closet, and the person at the controls faces you through a glass partition, communicating on intercom. Typ-ically, you record a take and then listen to a playback; then you record it again. When the casting director has what he wants, it's over. You might do a single take, or as many as eight or nine. There are rarely any callbacks, and performers are booked directly from these audition tapes.

Auditions for cartoon voices follow the same procedure except that most major producers in this arena, companies like Hanna-Barbera, have their own staff casting directors and recording booths, so they don't need to hire independent casting directors. The main difference between auditioning for this and radio or TV spots is that the casting director will talk to you in terms of character. "Okay, let's try the pig as French and see what happens" or "Can you make him more like a bank robber?" or "Make her older and fatter." This is a bit different from "Pick it up" or "Make it warmer, more smile" or "Just talk to me." It is where people who can create munchkins come into their glory.

Other types of voice work—slide/film narration, trailers for movies, recordings of books on tape—might be cast in the studios of independent casting directors, through agents, with auditions held in the offices of the employer, or with no auditions at all. Active producers continually accept and listen to performers' demo tapes, adding to the roster of names they can call.

HOW TO GET STARTED

The first thing you need to do is plug into the network of agents and workshops and have a demo tape made.

A good starting point would be to either conduct a telephone poll of a few voice agents (you can get a list from SAG or AFTRA) and ask for recommendations on workshops, or ask performers who are already working. Most of the workshops are conducted in recording studios and, since such small places can hold only a few people at a time, there might be a waiting list for the better ones. However, they are definitely the best entry point because you'll get a chance to work with the mike, to hear tapes of established performers, to network, and, on occasion, to be seen and heard by ad-agency producers and other employers of talent.

A commercial demo tape is three to five minutes long (three is better than five) and contains samples of your work. It is to voice talent what an 8 x 10 photo and resume is to on-camera talent. When you've been around long enough to have some spots on the air, you merely excerpt them, editing the pieces together on a single tape. Until then, you have to go into a studio and produce a demo from scratch, complete with sound effects and music. Ideally, a listener would conclude that the selections on your tape actually played on the air, so it's imperative that you put out a top-of-the-line product. You can't do it at home with your Sony cassette recorder.

An excellent producer, one experienced in assembling demo tapes, is a must, and you can find out who is good in your area by paying attention at the workshops. When you hear a good tape, ask who produced it. You'll hear the same names over and over. What you are looking for is a person who will help you select copy that shows you off to the best advantage and who will direct you in a recording session. Then he puts the tape together for you. Once you have a master tape in hand, you take it to a duplicating service to have as many copies as you want run off in reel-to-reel and cassette formats. Finally, you have to have stick-on labels made for the reel-to-reel copies and insert-style labels for the cassettes.

This can get expensive, as you might imagine. The last time I had a tape made and copied, complete with new labels, the bill exceeded $800. Depending on the sophistication of your labels, it could cost even more. Therefore, you need to be sure you start out right by getting the best producer. Warning: there are a lot of "producers" in the woods who will be happy to take your money. Be cautious! Only work with people on referral, and before you get involved with anybody, visit with them and listen to other tapes they have produced from scratch.

Before taking that step, however, get into a workshop and stay there a while. Most of the good ones cost no more than $35 per class. Spend some time listening, practicing, and learning. It is particularly important that you listen to the demo tapes of the performers who dominate the field so you can understand the competition. Only after you have done this and are firmly confident should you undertake the production of your own tape. I also suggest that you get a copy of *Word of Mouth: A Guide to Commercial Voice-over Excellence* by Susan Blu and Molly Ann Mullin (Pomegranate Press, Ltd., Los Angeles). It is a terrific primer, worth the purchase price for the glossary alone.

After you have a tape, set about finding an agent. Again, in the workshops, you'll find out rapidly which ones do the most work in town. Voice agents are generally receptive to receiving demo tapes and do listen to them. Because it doesn't take much time to toss a tape on a machine, and an in-person interview isn't necessary, it is relatively easier to get heard by a voice agent than it is to get seen by an on-camera agent.

You can also send your tape to independent casting directors and producers at ad agencies. Go to the library and look for the ''Red Book,'' the annual directory of ad agencies. It lists producers and other creative types, and indicates which products the agencies handle.

If you want to go after narration jobs, you might want to produce a demo tape specially for the purpose. It's okay to send your commercial demo tape to corporate film producers and companies that record books on tape, but it isn't up their alley. They have to use a bit of imagination to figure how you might sound with ten pages of straight dialogue or Chapter One of *Moby Dick*. You can probably connect with performers who do a lot of narration in the workshops, and you would do well to listen to their tapes before making one of your own.

A SOBERING POSTSCRIPT

The voice world, at least as it applies to commercials, is male-dominated. More than 80 percent of the voices in commercials are male, in fact. SAG and AFTRA have been active in trying to correct this imbalance, but we struggle against preconceived notions on Madison Avenue that male voices are more trust-inspiring, that they ''sell'' better. Progress is being made slowly, and the beat goes on.

6

Auditioning for TV Shows

Want some statistics? Try these on for size:

- Television consumes 23,000 hours of original programming each year.

- An episode of a typical prime-time action/adventure is shot in about a week.

- Daytime soap operas are usually shot at the incredible rate of one episode a day.

We're talking about a Marx Brothers frenzy here. The producers of a TV hit could well be responsible for delivering twenty episodes of their show in just about as many weeks. The wonder is that this pace allows for any quality at all.

Though there is a smattering of TV production in cities across the United States, particularly in New York, Chicago, and Boston, Hollywood remains the king of the mountain as a production center. In the heat of the season, during the fall and winter, casting sessions are held all over town, usually in small production offices on the various studio lots. Disney, Universal, 20th Century-Fox, Warner Brothers, and MGM are the lots where most of the action takes place.

When a Hollywood-based show shoots on location out-of-town, local actors are usually hired for the smaller roles as a cost cutting measure. It's cheaper to do that than it is to transport actors from Southern California, complete with per diem and hotel bills. Auditions for these smaller roles might be held anywhere, but are most apt to be held in makeshift production facilities of some kind. On occasion, they might be conducted in the offices of a local talent agent or independent casting director. Wherever they take place, the procedures are exactly the same as in Hollywood.

When I arrived on the West Coast in 1976, fresh from eight years on the New York stage and stock, I confess to being astonished at the way TV shows are cast. Shock number one was that actors in Hollywood have to audition for single-line roles. What can you do, after all, with "They went that-a-way!" in an audition? Probably because stage plays rarely have roles that small, I had never focused on the possibility that actors might have to take script in hand, stand up in front of the folks, and give a single line their best shot.

Shock number two was this business of "sides." The first time my agent arranged a reading for me and said that I could "pick up the sides any time before the audition," I hustled right over there, walked onto the Paramount lot, waved at the guards, found the production office, introduced myself to the receptionist . . . and was given two pages out of a script. "You are reading for Man 2 at the bar," she told me as I quickly scanned the pages. Sure enough, there were two lines for Man 2, one on the first page and one on the second. "Is there a complete script for this?" I asked. "No, the character is just in that one scene." "Oh." Again, with my stage background, I was ill-prepared for the way things are done in television-land.

The likelihood is that you, too, will begin your Hollywood days with these little roles, so be prepared. The only exceptions are for actors who arrive with entrée of some sort, people who manage to leap to a higher rung on the ladder and get top-level representation. If you've recently had the lead in a Broadway play and got boffo reviews, you're in luck. Catch a plane.

HOW TV SHOWS ARE CAST

Auditions for TV shows are conducted "live" about 97 percent of the time and are held in cramped production offices that have a living-room motif. Videotape is starting to find its way into the process, but it is so rarely used that it is almost not worth mentioning. The usual procedure is for the actor to read with a casting director in the presence of an assembled group of writers, producers, and the director. Unless the role is a major one, callbacks are nonexistent. You usually work within a week of that initial audition.

Unless you're working on a three-camera sitcom that will be shot in front of a live audience, you shouldn't anticipate any rehearsal time at all in TV. Actors are expected to have their lines committed to memory and to be ready to cook when they arrive on the set. Rehearsal consists of running things over with the director while the crew is setting up lights and camera. Frequently, you don't even know who the director is until he steps out of the crowd, introduces himself, and walks you through the scene.

If you come from a stage background, this way of working can be extremely unnerving. You always have the feeling that you are going off half-cocked, giving performances that are, to be charitable, somewhat lacking in depth. There is zero opportunity for exploration of your character, so you have to go with the most obvious choices.

The reason for this is the frantic production pace I mentioned. Everybody is running to keep up in this business. The networks make their program purchases in early summer, usually the month of May, and that leaves producers only a matter of weeks to get into production. Shows have to be ready for the start of the fall season, remember. In an ideal world, they would love to rehearse and make nice art, but there simply isn't any time. The dynamic is more like a bunch of runners popping out of the starting gate.

This fact of television life has dramatic implications for the actor in the audition room. Because there isn't going to be any time for rehearsal, they want to see precisely what you plan to do when you show up on the set. In short, they want to see the performance.

Think about this now: in a commercial, you're only dealing with a framework of thirty seconds at most, and they are going to shoot that same thirty seconds over and over and over again until they get exactly what they want. Therefore, it isn't necessary to show *the* performance in audition. Your scene in a TV show, on the other hand, is likely to be only one of several that must be shot on the same day. You aren't going to get the chance to do it again and again. You'll get one take, maybe two, sometimes three, and they'll do enough angles to allow for editing choices. A master, a couple of close-ups, and "bye bye."

Television puts a high premium on a fast-study, one-take actor, the kind of person who is willing to leap to performance and willing to do precisely the things that a good acting teacher will pin your ears for. I once heard someone describe acting on TV as "not acting at all, but rather, something like acting," and I don't think he was far off the mark.

Auditions call for the strongest possible choices from actors, and sometimes you can come out smelling like a rose with choices that have nothing to do with the character. I once went to a Broadway audition and performed Lucky's speech from *Waiting For Godot* backward, last word first, first word last. They loved it, and I got called back.

TV is another matter, and you have to tread carefully. Yes, make strong choices, but watch out that you don't make strange ones. Whatever you do in the audition room should be within the realm of what you will do if you get hired. These guys do not want surprises. They want reassurance. They do not delight in the unknown, and they aren't looking forward to a rehearsal process in which we all get together and work it out. They want to know what you plan to do and, if they hire you, want you to do precisely that when you work.

THREE-CAMERA VS. EPISODIC VS. SOAP OPERAS

A distinction should be made between three-camera sitcoms, typically videotaped in front of a live audience, and episodic programs, usually shot on 35mm film on sound stages and location. The former, in fairness, does have something resembling rehearsal, a sort of souped-up one-week summer stock. The cast is assembled on Monday, rehearses through the week, and tapes on Friday. They still want to see the performance at the audition, though, because much of the rehearsal involves making scenes work for the camera, rather than shaping content and interpretation. Soap operas operate on a production schedule of one show per day, so the concept of rehearsal is also amusing: you show up in the morning, go through it three or four times, and then tape in the afternoon. For soap opera auditions, they want the same thing—the performance.

THE CURSE OF SIDES

For the casting director, sides are a great convenience and cost-saving device. All he does is photocopy the specific pages that each character appears in and let the actors audition using those instead of an entire script. If the character appears in several different scenes scattered through the script, then he excerpts all of those scenes and staples them together.

For the actor, sides present a triple whammy. As any self-respecting stage actor knows, characters do not stand alone. They interrelate with other characters and with situations. Anybody who has ever studied with Uta Hagen or Stella Adler knows how to break down a script to come up with an intelligent analysis. We learn that it is something close to a mortal sin to pull a monologue out of context in a play and simply commit it to memory. Well, welcome to La La Land, the place where rules of convention are turned on their head.

To give you an idea of how awkward it can be to audition with sides: not too long ago, I was up for a nice role in a hit show produced by Universal. The character owned a jewelry store, and there was a robbery. Three scenes were involved.

The first scene establishes the relationship between the owner and his assistant: this is a quality jewelry store, not a pawn shop. Suddenly, the robbers run in, two of them with guns drawn. "Everybody lay on the floor!" they order as they snatch jewels from shelves and stuff them in their bags. Without warning, one of the robbers turns at the door and shoots the prone assistant in the back, killing him instantly. They flee as burglar alarms scream. Scene number two has the star of the show talking quietly and sympathetically with the distraught store owner. Scene number three takes place several days later down at the police station: question and answer time. By this time, the owner is subdued and rather depressed, no longer hysterical.

In the audition, the casting director read all of the parts except mine, making it necessary for me to jump in when it was my turn. More important, however, she went directly from one scene to the next without a moment of transition. There was no way for me, with the owner's part, to make adjustments to incorporate all of the violence and mayhem. There I was, screaming "You killed him!" at the robbers and then, spinning on a dime, I had to be immediately distraught in the scene with the hero. Spinning again, I had to mentally cut to two days later, flinging myself into a depressed reading. It was enough to give an actor nosebleed.

Was it a fair audition? Did the producers get an accurate idea of what I might do with the role? Not really, because on the actual job, though there wouldn't be time for rehearsal, I would have time to consider the transitions. The scenes might not even be shot on the same day. This audition was absolutely typical, however, and every other actor out there in the waiting room had to go through the same mess. I didn't get that particular role.

Why do they do that? Why put actors through a wringer audition? Simple. Just as they don't have any time to rehearse, they also don't have any time to cast. They have six or thirteen or twenty episodes to shoot, are already two weeks off-schedule because the star has the flu, and we're just coming out of a strike. Casting is just one more hassle to have to hurry up and deal with. From where the executives are sitting, an actor who has to be nursed along with such niceties as transition time and rehearsal probably won't be able to work at the pace demanded by TV anyway.

PREPARING FOR THE AUDITION

Check in with the receptionist when you arrive. If you haven't already received sides, she'll give them to you. There are none of those official SAG sign-in sheets like you see at commercial auditions. Also, since far fewer actors are seen for these roles than are seen for commercials, you don't have to worry about being kept too long in the waiting room. It is rare that you will have to wait longer than thirty minutes before being called in.

Your audition will almost certainly involve a dialogue situation of some kind, so there is not much to be gained by talking to light switches in preparation for it. Instead, you should spend your time considering clear, strong choices that will propel you into the reading and carry you through. Look for subtext, conflict, relationship, humor.

Personally, I like to get away from the other actors in the waiting room so that I'm not distracted. It's okay to ask the receptionist to look for you in the hallway when they are ready for you. She'll come and get you. Stay away from mirrors (unless you are laughing at yourself in them) for the same reason as I gave in the commercial section: you can't be the actor and the audience simultaneously.

Be aware that time will fly in the audition room, so you want to do everything you can to gain control of the situation. If you can, pick up the sides in advance of the audition so you can see what kind of monster you are dealing with. Pay particular attention to the page numbers—that is the easiest way to tell if you are going to be reading multiple scenes. Take a hi-lighter or magic marker and underline your lines— you won't have to return the sides, and under the tension in the audition room, the script can become a blur. Bold markings can be your personal road map. Be sure to mark transition points clearly so you can see them under pressure.

Create a context for each scene, even if you are not sure it is correct. Examine the relationship between the characters.

Are they friends? Don't know? Could they be? Fine. They're friends, then, What time of day does the scene occur? Is the character tired or alert? if your character has a scene with the lead of the show, count your blessings, and create the relationship. Is there any way in the world that the star and your character could know one another, be friends? If so, go for it. It's better to sin on the side of familiarity. Maybe it will give the writers the bright idea to put this "friend" back into another episode.

Give yourself a strong motivation for each scene, something that will really propel you. What does your character want in this scene? Or, put a better way, what do *I* want in this scene? (When working on a role, it is best to refer to your character in the first person right from the start. It breaks down the distance, helps you "own" it quickly.)

Use substitution if the scenes don't have a context that invites color and depth. In the jewelry store robbery, I pretended that the assistant who got killed was my real-life brother, Richard. The people watching the reading didn't know the difference, but the substitution gave me something stronger to react to when the robbers shot him. It also helped raise the stakes for the next scene, where I had to be so distraught.

Be familiar with the format of the show, if at all possible. I make it a personal policy to watch at least one episode of every new show each season—no matter how awful it might be. It is best to have a "feel" for a show at the audition, and you can't always get that from the sides.

Look for ways your character can emotionally "turn corners" during the reading. I'm not talking about major transitions, but subtle ones. If there is any way, for example, to have the character start the scene laughing and end the scene somber, do it.

THE AUDITIONING PROCESS

In TV auditions, the auditors are usually no more than five to ten feet from you, so there is no need to project. You'll read with the casting director, but the actual director will give any adjustments. You may go through it once or twice, usually just once, and then it's all over. One advantage of having the auditors so close to you is that you can get a good sense of whether or not they like what you are doing. I recall that my first audition for ''The Fall Guy'' was on a day when things weren't going well. After performing the scene twice, I knew the next words out of the director's mouth would be ''thank you,'' but I also knew I didn't have the part, so I suggested that perhaps I could try something wild with the scene. The auditors looked at one another, and the director said to go ahead. I then went way out on a limb, further than I normally would in a TV audition, and it worked. The character was extreme, a real mental case, and when I extended it, something clicked; I got the role. The producer of that show was one of the busiest producers in Hollywood. He saw what I did that day, and ever since, he has simply hired me with no audition. I have now worked on many of his shows—and it all came from reading the faces in that audition room. Here are a few pointers for auditioning:

Remember to use humor. These pressure-cooker situations send humor flying right out the window. If you can find any way at all to justify it, smile, laugh, and chuckle. Play opposites.

When they offer you a chair, scoot it a few inches one way or the other. They've gotten used to seeing actor after actor in that chair. By moving it, you ''own'' it and are subtly taking charge of the room.

Keep the script in your hand even if you have memorized the part. Refer to it from time to time. Even though there isn't going to be any rehearsal, the implication is that, if you are this wonderful with a script in your hand, just imagine how extraordinary your performance will be once you have had time to get off script.

When reading, make eye contact with the casting director as much as possible. Don't bury your head in the script.

Try to control the pace of the scene. The casting director will probably read too fast, and you can usually break the rhythm when you are speaking. Look for ways to pause mid-sentence, to reflect, to shift your intention. If you control the pace, the auditors will hang on your every word. It is another way of "taking stage," or controlling the room.

Never, ever touch the casting director.

Since the casting director is going to be reading all of the parts except yours, find ways to differentiate between the characters. The casting director is likely to deliver the lines of the robbers pretty much like the lines of the cops, but you should know to relate to the cops and robbers in different ways.

Controlling the pace of the scene is a good thing to do but, in general, good actors want to take *too* many dramatic pauses. Therefore, unless you are purposely trying to break the pace set by the casting director, use this device sparingly. In life, we tend to perk along, and that will ring truest in a reading.

Feel free to get up and move around if you want. The chair is there for your convenience. Be careful, though, that you don't get caught up in aimless pacing. Also, remember that these audition rooms are usually quite small and cramped. There isn't much place to travel. If a scene calls for your character to enter the room, you might want to stand at the office door and, as you begin, turn to face the group. That will give you the option of doing the scene standing or sitting.

Acting is about *doing* something, right? We learn in acting classes that acting has very little to do with words. You know it, and I know it, but for some reason, many people who write for TV apparently don't. They tend to put in too much expository talking and ho-hum filler. Many of the supporting roles that you will audition for seem to exist for no other reason than to provide the lead of the show with some tidbit of information. For example, the need will arise to somehow communicate to the lead the news that the prime suspect has moved out of his apartment. Easy! Let's just invent a cleaning woman and let her tell him about it. The actor comes into the audition and finds himself with two pages of pure exposition to render. Lots of names, addresses and times—dull, dull, dull.

The trick is to bring an attitude to such roles, a context, or a reason for living that is not in the script. Maybe this is the fourth time this week that the cleaning woman has had to answer questions about this particular tenant, and she's getting darned tired of it. Or maybe the cleaning woman thinks this particular cop is cute. Or maybe he reminds her of her own son. Maybe she harbors a secret desire to be a detective herself, so when she starts telling about the suspect moving out, she does so with a conspiratorial tone. Get it? Try to find some place to hang your hat with a character. Another line of wisdom I've heard in the street is that, with TV scripts, the writers provide the situation, but it's up to the actor to provide the character. Again, not far off the mark.

Now, a special comment about those one- and two-line roles, the kind you audition for with a single sheet of paper, "They went that-a-way!" parts. They pay the bills, and at the beginning you are going to do them. Remember this, however: the show is not about the fellow who yells "They went that-a-way!" Don't overdo it in the audition room. Don't try to make it into something that it's not, because you'll just scare the producers. For example, if you were up for the role of a waitress, and your only line was "Be with you in a minute, Sir," you wouldn't want to deliver it as if you and the star of the show had had a lover's quarrel and you are avoiding him now. You wouldn't want to stare daggers at him. Just get busy with your waitressing, justify your choices in terms of restaurant activity, and do your job.

EPISODES, PILOTS, AND MOVIES-OF-THE-WEEK

The workaday money for actors in Hollywood comes from episodic TV shows (plus commercials, of course). These shows are great because you get paid to shoot the show, and then you get paid 100 percent of that when it runs again in summer rerun. And you get paid when the show goes into syndication. And you get paid again when it is sold overseas, though by this point your checks are down to about $8.46 per episode. Virtually everybody pushes and shoves to get work on the hit shows for this reason.

Pilots are another story. They aren't worth all that much unless they are picked up by a network. This is highly unlikely, but if a pilot is picked up, and if you have a good role in one, then you'll wind up as a regular on the show. If the show turns out to be a hit, which is even more unlikely, then you get to move to Boardwalk and start collecting $10,000+ per segment. It's about the same odds as hitting the lottery.

The starring roles in pilots, and the major guest-star roles on episodics and sitcoms, generally go to a pool of actors who are already "known" in the industry. Frequently, they don't have to audition. Instead, they "take meetings," and their agents send their demo reels around for the execs to check out. It's a different ballgame, one we all want to play in. If actors in this group do have to endure auditions, they are generally treated with more respect than "day players." They are given complete scripts in advance and scheduled ample audition time. It's sort of like the difference between flying first-class and tourist.

If you have the good fortune to land an audition for a strong role in a pilot, and if the producers like you, you will probably have to read several times. After you clear the producers and writers, you have to pass muster with the network, and you might even have to go through a screen test. After casting is narrowed down to a few possible candidates, negotiations are held with each actor's agent just in case he is chosen. Contracts are signed for a series deal, contingent upon final casting. That way, a performer who is chosen for a good role can't turn around and say to the producers, "Want me, huh? Well, it's going to cost you $18 million!" The contracts have already been signed, sealed, and delivered.

Movies-of-the-week are like little feature films with spaces for commercials, and auditioning for them is just like going up for an episodic. The average budget is a bit over $2.5 million, compared to the $8 to $16 million for a feature film, and they take about 20 days to shoot. Many movies-of-the-week are barely-disguised trial balloons for possible series.

BILLING

This is one of the really silly facets of television. Billing is a negotiable item. Theoretically, a *featured* role is the smallest kind you can play, *co-star* is the next step up, and *guest star* is the highest rung on the ladder short of being a regular on the show. You would think that the size of the part has a mathematical and inflexible relationship to the billing on the screen—that if someone is billed as a co-star, that means he is playing a true lead. In Hollywood, there is no such logic. The way the game is played is this: when you are hired to play a role, your agent has to negotiate both money and billing with the casting director, who operates within parameters already set by the show's producers. In the case of large roles, true guest-star parts, the whole thing is easy. Billing is guest-star billing, and money is "top of the show."

With the smaller supporting roles, the box starts losing its shape. Whatever you got paid on your last job is your "rate" or "quote," and the unspoken law of the jungle is that the present employer is going to pay at least the same. When you hear an actor say, "They are paying my rate," that's what he means.

But suppose you got paid $1,000 a day on your last job and got co-star billing; and suppose that the present job isn't as big as the last one you did, isn't worth $1,000 a day. Suppose the casting director is offering $800 a day and featured billing. Your agent might respond by saying, "Well, she really wants to do this show, so we'll take the $800 on a 'no-quote' basis, but we have to have co-star billing." If the casting director agrees, what they are saying is that the current show will pay less than your rate, but nobody will tell, so the higher amount you got on your previous job remains your quote. Isn't this wonderful? Stanislavski would be turning over in his grave.

It is possible to negotiate better billing than a role is in fact worth, particularly if the money is not there. Once you crack the guest-star barrier, however, it would be something close to a mortal sin to work in a featured part, would be a testament to your failing career. Oh, you might fudge and accept a co-star role, but never a featured one. Even if you were doing a favor for the producer of the show by accepting a two-line part, you could not accept featured billing because you officially work at the guest-star level. Mind you, none of this is actually written down anywhere. It is just common knowledge in the biz.

Another negotiable item is *where* your billing appears. The best place is in the opening credits because viewers are theoretically paying more attention then. And it is highly desirable to have a "separate card," meaning that your name appears on screen by itself. If you don't negotiate a separate card, then your name will appear on a "shared card" with other actors' names. Perish the thought. Featured billing invariably appears in the end credits, as does co-star most of the time. Opening credits are usually reserved for star billing, major guest stars, and regulars.

The least desirable billing, the absolute bottom of the barrel, is "end credits at producer's discretion." That means your name may or may not show up at all and, if it does, it will surely be buried in the end credits that go by so fast no one except you and your mom will notice.

There are variables on all of this, but you get the idea. The balloon I want to burst here is the idea that there is a correlation between the size of the part and billing on TV. It's all highly negotiable.

THE FUTURE OF TELEVISION

Don't look now, but television is changing. The networks have battle fatigue. Their share of the total viewing audience has slipped from 92 percent in 1978 to less than 75 percent in 1987. Even *Life* magazine, in its 21st-century projections, is predicting the demise of networks as we know them. Already, Hollywood is producing 65 to 70 movies-of-the-week for the networks each year and 40 to 50 for cable, a significantly narrow margin. Networks are having to compete with much racier programming, and they fight an uphill battle against the VCR/rental-movie market. Also, the independent stations are getting stronger and have better shows than they used to have when TV was more heavily regulated by the government. When the networks do get people to sit still and watch, they have to contend with remote-control devices that make it possible for viewers to zip from one station to the next and to zap commercials. One recent study indicated that viewers with remote-control devices are only seeing 50 percent of the commercials, and from the networks' perspective, this is not happy news.

When ratings go down, advertising dollars drop. And as a result of that, the networks pay producers less to deliver their shows (licensing fees), and they order fewer episodes. This puts the producers in the hot seat because network licensing fees have never fully covered all production costs. Producers deficit-finance on the hope that their show will be a hit so they can turn around and sell it into syndication and make real bucks. The network fees only give the network the right to air a show twice and, after that, the rights revert back to the producers.

Enter *first-run syndication*, the wave of the future. Producers are discovering that it can be more worthwhile financially to bypass the networks altogether and to produce programs directly for all of those little independent stations around the country. What they do is make a pilot, shop it around to the independent stations, take orders for episodes from each depending on what the market will bear, and then, based on the orders, borrow the money to produce the shows. It is kind of like the garment business, and the procedure is turning television inside out. Every major studio now has a division that is devoted to nothing except producing and selling shows into first-run syndication. An added bonus is that the producers aren't fettered by network censors, and these new shows are frequently more inventive and stimulating than what is on network.

This movement, combined with the blossoming of cable television and its appetite for original programming, is bound to change the shape of the medium. For one thing, programs can be targeted to smaller audiences. It is a fact that, on network, a show that attracts only twenty million viewers is a flop, but in first-run is a sizable hit. For another thing, production seasons are starting to blur. The only reason we have a fall start for new shows on network is that the time coincides with the introduction of the new line of cars in Detroit. First-run and cable won't be affected by that, and production will spread more evenly year round.

Auditioning for first-run is just like any other TV audition, except that the producers are always crying poor because they don't have network bucks behind them, using that as an excuse to pay you less. That will work itself out in time.

The most important implication for actors in all of this is the likelihood that Hollywood will lose its hold as *the* production center. Already, producers are looking to Canada and states like North Carolina and Florida to shoot their shows because costs are lower. With first-run, it is only a matter of time until cities like Chicago, Detroit, and San Francisco begin functioning as program sources. All the work doesn't have to come from Hollywood. It's not carved in stone anywhere; it's that way only because most production has traditionally be controlled by the studios and networks. By the turn of the century, TV as you and I know it will appear quaint. As they say, nothing is constant except change.

7

Auditioning for Movies

Is there really such a creature as a "film actor" as opposed to a "stage actor" or "TV actor"? Before I moved to the West Coast, I harbored the romantic notion of the actor as a traveling player, and would have dismissed this question as being out of hand. Art was what it was all about, and that began and ended right under the proscenium arch. From my perspective, movies were about commerce, kleig lights, moguls, palm trees—anything but art. Sure, you had your occasional *On The Waterfront* or *Rebel Without A Cause*, but essentially, movies equalled Hollywood, and Hollywood equalled Doris Day. Television was only good for the income to be earned from commercials, and that was something you did so you could keep doing plays. Now, after spending thirteen years immersed in a world of Nielsen ratings and screenings instead of New York opening nights, I can't be quite so smug. I still cling to the belief that acting is an art form, but I've learned that the art is in the person, not in the media. Working actors regularly shift back and forth between TV, film, and stage with no accompanying loss of integrity. The interesting thing is how some performers seem to glow on film while others seem to be ideally suited to TV or stage. Why is that? Could it be that there really is something called a "film actor?" And why do some actors become movie stars while others get their own TV series?

Walter Kerr wrote a marvelous article some years back in the *New York Times* in which he observed that a "larger-than-life" quality seems to be inherent in many stage stars. He cited Carol Channing as someone who, if you met her on the street, would appear to be an amalgamation of disparate features: a very large mouth, extremely big eyes, a voice of unusual distinction. But on stage, all of that blends into a whole that perfectly bridges the gap between actor and audience. I think he was on to something. Though he didn't say so, Miss Channing is an uncomfortable fit on the big screen; the very factors that serve as her assets on stage are liabilities when everything is amplified mechanically. In fact, some of the finest actors in this country simply don't translate well to film.

Why is it that someone like James Dean was such a natural movie actor? Why John Wayne and Joan Crawford? Michael J. Fox and John Ritter, though they both star in movies, seem to best fit on the TV screen. Tom Selleck and Alan Alda swing back and forth between TV and movies, and sell lots of tickets with their names over the title. Yet even though they have successfully capitalized on TV fame in order to work in features, they are still essentially TV people. Goldie Hawn, on the other hand, made the leap from TV to film, but for some reason, you *don't* think of her as a TV person. Irene Worth, Uta Hagen and Joel Grey rarely venture far from the theater, where they are major stars.

What's the variable? Not raw talent—if it were, then Angela Lansbury and Hal Linden, among many others, would be known as movie stars rather than stage or TV stars. It isn't merely a matter of where a performer gets his first break: Clint Eastwood first worked on TV, but there is no question he is a top-of-the-pile movie star. It's not because some actors get that perfect showcase role, and others don't. The ground is littered with performers who soared into stardom with their first movies, only to tumble right back down, unable to sustain careers in the medium. And it's definitely not a matter of good looks—otherwise, how do you explain Charles Bronson?

Movies and stage have something in common that TV doesn't share, and that may be the key to the puzzle: neither answers directly to Madison Avenue. As we have already discussed, a non-threatening sense of life is a critical ingredient for people who act in commercials, and since TV as a medium pretty much exists to deliver good-humored consumers to the advertisers, maybe that same dynamic is essential to actors who work on TV in general. Movies and stage, by contrast, answer only to the ticket purchaser, and though they aim to entertain, they don't necessarily have to keep the audience in a mood to buy something. There are movie stars like Bette Midler who have a non-threatening, basically friendly dynamic, but most of the major names have an air of unpredictability, even danger. Think of De Niro, James Woods, Hoffman, Nicholson, Jane Fonda, and Brando. When they make their rare appearances on TV, they are out of their element, too hot to handle, in a manner of speaking. They carry enough voltage to blow out the fuse box.

I recently had a conversation with a movie casting director in Hollywood, and in answer to this question about movie actors versus TV actors, she said that she could tell in a first meeting if an actor will work best on TV or in movies. How? She didn't know. A hunch, maybe, a sense that a particular actor has an off-center quality or look that will work well on the big screen.

What I've finally come around to is this: yes, there is such a thing as a "film actor," if you mean someone whose appearance and personality synthesize perfectly in movies in a way that they don't on stage or TV. Some actors literally go through an ugly duckling/lovely swan transformation in the medium and become stars. By the same token, there are actors who seem incomplete unless they are standing on the legitimate stage. Like Olivier, when they make their entrance, the lights seem to get brighter. They belong there. However, all of this is absolutely beyond the actor's control, so you might as well just concentrate on the work. No matter how much film technique you develop, how skilled you become at working with the camera, film will either enhance you or it won't. If it doesn't, it isn't the end of the world, because you can still act in movies, can still play major leads in them. It only means that you aren't likely to be catapulted into the ranks of actors who are paid millions of dollars for making movies. The movies will be a place you visit rather than a place where you live. Farrah Fawcett may star in movies, but she is not a movie star; Marilyn Monroe was a movie star.

As for whether or not you might be a "TV actor," it comes down to that non-threatening sense of life, and again, there isn't much you can do about it. Because TV reaches into the homes of 40 million people at one time, and because advertisers are paying for the whole transaction, there definitely is a premium put on performers who are not going to offend or otherwise alienate consumers.

HOW MOVIES ARE CAST

The best way to get a handle on movie casting is to contrast the medium to TV. Consider, for example, the different budgets. The average studio-produced feature film now costs about $16 million, and the average independent feature one-third of that. Compare these figures to the following TV costs: a movie-of-the-week runs about $2.5 million; a one-hour segment of a prime-time episodic, about $1.2 million; a half-hour sitcom is in the $400,000 range; one episode of a soap opera, about $75,000; a game show, maybe $30,000.

What this means is that in the movies, you have an awful lot of money being used to produce an hour and a half of celluloid. That in itself doesn't guarantee excellence, but it does assure a lot of attention to detail, starting with scripts and ending with casting , and it marks a striking difference between TV and movies. As we've already seen, television operates on a frantic agenda. A two-hour movie-of-the-week might be shot on a twenty-day schedule, but a feature film that length could easily take twice or three times as long. Moviemakers tend to lovingly craft their films, turning out one-of-a-kind works of art.

And then there is the element of magic, that intangible that makes movies a heart-stopper for most actors. The medium is thrilling, full of romance and mystery, played out against a universe-wide panorama, evoking memories of childhoods spent in darkened halls watching James Dean and Bette Davis. Movies are a more exotic form than TV, and this fact of life colors the entire production procedure. To a fly on the wall, a casting session for a movie looks identical to one for a TV show, but there are differences—hard to define, perhaps, but there nonetheless.

The casting director for a movie has a much closer relationship with the director than does his counterpart on TV. Directors come and go on television shows; they are typically hired for two or three episodes, while the show itself lives on. The casting director is part of the production team that is in place before a director is hired, and works more for the show than the director. Indeed, the casting director might not even be certain who the director is for next week's episode when he begins pre-screening and preparing cast lists.

A *movie* casting director is hired for a single project, and before he sees his first actor, he will have long talks with the director in which they discuss tone, style, maybe even the director's working methods. When I was casting the film version of Nathaniel West's book *Miss Lonelyhearts*, the director was insistent that I bring in actors who projected a certain "emptiness." He wanted to capture the grays of the Depression era in Los Angeles, envisioning a movie full of long shadows, dusks, and lonely dawns; the actors had to fit in, even those in the smallest roles. By the time I started pre-screening, I was really an extension of the director's inner vision.

The closest equivalent in television to this kind of careful casting process would be in movies-of-the-week, but the budget doesn't allow for a lot of pre-production time, and anyway, directors and casting directors are bound by such considerations as TV Q, the quasi-secret coding system that measures actors' popularity with the TV audience. It is not unusual for a director of a movie-of-the-week to be given a list of "approved" actors from which to select his leads.

Next to arranging financing for the project and signing up stars, the most important decision a movie producer has to make is the hiring of the director. Once the director comes on board, he is the general/leader, and the production is tailored to his specifications. He usually brings with him his own immediate production staff, including an assistant director and cinematographer, and he frequently chooses his own casting director. Compared to television, in which the director rides along with the production, in a movie, the director *is* the ride. His vision is the one that is expected to be up on the screen.

I'm not naive. I realize there are some mega-stars that have more power than most religious leaders; on *their* movies, everything is put together to fit their tastes. Such a star might well have final say on all casting and might even have the "final cut" in editing. He likely has a hand in hiring the director, too, but there are only a few of these creatures, surely less than ten in the whole industry, and we do not need to include them or their projects in this discussion.

If you can compare the producer's optioning a script or a novel to selecting a song, then hiring the director is like employing someone who will both arrange the song and select the musicians and singers. What the director wants filters down through the ranks in a very specific way, right into the casting sessions.

The mechanics of the movie-casting session are identical to those for the TV-casting session. The actors read from sides (as opposed to complete scripts) with the casting director in front of a group that includes the director, and may also include producers and a writer, though screenwriters have less to do with casting than TV writers. Usually, once a producer has optioned a script, the writer is out of the picture. Videotape is seldom used in these casting sessions, and screen tests may be required for larger roles.

ACTING FOR MOVIES

"I thought acting was acting was acting no matter where you might do it," I can almost hear you say. That's right, it is. But then, you can travel from Santa Fe to Los Angeles by bus, car, train, or airplane, can't you? They will all get you from one place to the next, are all forms of transportation . . . but they're different.

In the beginning, there was the stage. The actor and the audience got together in the same place at the same time, and the actor had the responsibility of making sure that every member of the audience could see and hear what was going on. Given that a person sitting more than halfway back in an amphitheater might not be able to pick up the subtle shifts in an actor's eyes, might not see the twitch of a cheek, the actor had to adjust to compensate for the distance.

Then came movies, a medium in which the actor's performance is carried to the audience through mechanical means. The actor no longer had to concern himself with compensation for distance, his performance being extraordinarily amplified on the screen. A lifted eyebrow becomes a major event in extreme closeup, when your face is twenty feet tall. That's why the wisdom in movies is that "if you think something, it is done." You don't need to "do" as much as you do on stage. Yes, you need to play your action—and do all of the things a good performance on stage would demand—but you don't need to take it to the audience. For someone from a stage background, this is a real adjustment to make. It is hard to trust the camera at first, and you always have the feeling that you aren't doing enough.

You may have heard it said that "acting is reacting." Though this may be a generally useful perspective, on film it is really imperative. The next time you watch a movie, notice how they always cut to reaction shots. For example, you may see a child dart into the street chasing a ball. Then, a quick cut to an extreme closeup of a woman driving a car. We see her react to the child, slamming on the brakes, horrified. Or say a beautiful woman enters the room at a party, pausing at the door. The director may well cut to a reaction shot of a very interested man. We know immediately what he thinks of the woman, whether he knows her or not, whether he admires her beauty. Reaction, reaction, reaction. Yes, acting is "doing," but in the movies, you do less and react more.

I saw a graphic example of this while teaching a series of summer workshops on Acting For Camera. The purpose of the classes was to explore the differences between acting for stage versus acting for film, and the participants were, for the most part, highly experienced stage actors. Sprinkled among them were a few newcomers.

Scenes were assigned, rehearsed, and then videotaped, complete with master shots, reverses, the works. Then we studied the results. Surprisingly, the new people frequently came off better than some of the old pros. Why? At first, we were mystified by it, but then, in a flash, it became clear: the new people didn't have enough craft yet to know about propelling a scene along! They only knew to stay in the present moment and to react. The experienced actors would aggressively pursue their objectives, and if teamed with less experienced actors, would try to compensate for what they perceived the newcomers were not doing. On stage, they would have gotten away with it, but on film, they appeared uncentered. They seemed to be flailing.

Now, let me hasten to add that reacting rather than acting is decidedly not synonymous with having no energy. I have seen actors so concerned about doing too much for film that they managed to project a repressed dynamic. They seemed energy-less and, worse, boring. Movies are not grim, and directors love actors with a good sense of humor and energy. You do not have to "act small" for a film. On the contrary, you should care passionately and deeply about what is going on in the scene. The trick is to be honest 100 percent of the time, because the camera will detect the slightest lapse in concentration.

HELPFUL HINTS

Here are some special tips for auditioning for movies:

- You can presume the casting director is intimately familiar with the roles in the script and has a pre-determined idea of what the director wants. Ask questions at a pre-screen audition if you want to. Deal with the casting director of a movie in the same fashion you might if you were talking to the actual director.

- If you are naturally animated (as I am), remember to calm down a bit for film. Jumpy, jerky, helter-skelter movement might work great on stage, but on film, it is a killer. Internalize. Same passion, just internalize. Yul Brynner once advised a new actor to ''practice stillness.'' Good advice.

- A movie director is influenced by an actor's personality, and will likely take the time to chat with you. Be honest, not defensive. He is just trying to get to know you. The camera sees everything, remember.

- By all means, show the director the actual performance. There may be a limited rehearsal period for the leads of the film, but supporting players are expected to show up on the set ready to cook, just like in TV. The difference is that in movies, the director has the luxury of doing more takes than TV, so there is not as much pressure as a rule.

- If you have a theatrical ''reel,'' take it with you to every movie audition. TV directors are usually too rushed to look at them, but an interested movie director just might.

THE FUTURE OF MOVIES

The burgeoning number of multiplex theaters, combined with the importance of the videocassette market, guarantee an escalation in the number of relatively low-budget independent movies, with big movies like *Star Wars* sprinkled in sparsely. The days of the huge studio with hundreds of actors under contract are long gone. The studios remain in name only, now being owned by massive conglomerates such as Gulf & Western and Coca-Cola. True, they are still producing movies, but more and more, they are merely distributing movies that other people make. In 1987, more than 40 percent of the Academy Award nominations went to movies that were neither made nor distributed by the eight major studios.

Movies like *The Whales of August, Talk Radio, Sammy and Rosie Get Laid, Dirty Dancing*, and *Wish You Were Here* are good examples of the direction the industry is taking. A film like *She's Gotta Have It* only cost $200,000 to produce, and *River's Edge* cost just over $1 million. Even the gorgeous *Room With A View* only ran a bit over $3 million. Because the producers aren't saddled with huge studio overhead, costs for such things as backlots and soundstages, they are able to "put all of the money up on the screen." The multiplex theaters have a voracious appetite for new movies, a demand that can't begin to be met by major studios, and the videocassette market is ever ready to chip in a million or so for a movie's cost in exchange for early rights. In fact, some companies that were formed for the purpose of videocassette distribution have begun producing their own movies from scratch.

Though movie production is still centered in Hollywood, it is bound to decentralize, and this is good news for actors. There will be more movies made, costing less money, distributed more widely than ever before, and coming from more eclectic sources. The world is getting smaller.

8

Auditioning for Industrial/Educational Films

The Screen Actors Guild Industrial/Educational contract covers just about everything that isn't a feature film, television show, commercial, or music video. At your local videotape rental store, all of those tapes on health, fitness, beauty tips, and wine tasting were probably produced under this contract, as were those department-store videos playing next to the makeup counter. This category is one of the fastest developing of all. Since 1984, combined SAG and AFTRA earnings under the contract have skyrocketed from $4.8 million to $22 million, and the best is yet to come.

By far the biggest boom is happening in corporate applications of films for training, public relations, and sales promotions. Eighty percent of all companies that have programs for educating their employees include video seminars in the curriculum. Companies like GTE, Safeway Stores, and IBM regularly employ actors for training films—which, by the way, are misleadingly named, since 95 percent of them are shot on videotape.

There are basically two kinds of producers making films for corporate use. The first produces generic films on such subjects as good employee relations, office manners, and proper dental hygiene; these films are available on a rental basis to whatever companies want them. The second kind of producer makes films for the internal use of specific companies, perhaps instructing new employees how to operate a computer, wire a panel, or prepare a division report. From the actor's perspective, this second kind is full of audition land mines. Since they won't be seen by the general public, such films are full of seemingly cryptic corporate jargon. Reading for them reminds me of exercises I used to do in acting class involving the Jabberwock speech in *Alice In Wonderland*. The idea was to act out various everyday scenarios, like buying the groceries and getting the car fixed while speaking only the nonsense words from the book. I have acted in corporate films in which I understood no more than 30 percent of what I was saying. The following sample script will illustrate the challenge:

FADE IN to discover BOB and CARL in a hotel room. They are bent over some papers which are spread on the coffee table in front of them.

BOB

I really appreciate you taking this time with me, Carl. This DDAT proposal is the biggest project I've handled, and you are an expert in this area.

CARL

That's all right, Bob. Happy to help. You already have the basics, and if I can go over the format revisions with you, I think you'll come out smelling like a rose. Let's start with Phase I, OK?

BOB

Great! That's my biggest problem.

CARL

No sweat. You worked on the Pre-Allocation System, didn't you?

BOB

Sure. We all did.

CARL

Right. Well, Phase I actually came from the things we learned on that job. . . .

BOB

You mean, this is an extension of the Random Walk work
that Lois and the fellows at BALCOM were doing?

CARL

Exactly. Let's take this first set of figures because they
come directly from the PAS job.

You see the problem? This type of material presupposes all
manner of knowledge that an actor can't be expected to have.
What on earth is a "Pre-Allocation System," anyway? Is
"DDAT" a kind of bug spray? The people who are going to
watch the film know what all that means, so the actor has to
pretend he does, too. Unlike the situation with strange commercial copy, you can't ask for quick explanations at the
audition. You just have to wing it.

THE AUDITIONING PROCESS

Auditions for industrial/educational films, or corporate
films, are typically videotaped, just like those for commercials. They might be held in the studios of an independent
casting director, or at a production company. Outside of L.A.
and New York, you might even read in the offices of a talent
agent. The audition may be conducted by a casting director
or by the actual director, and, as with auditions for TV shows
and movies, you read from sides instead of complete scripts.

Always wear clothes that are appropriate for an office
when you go to these auditions, unless you are specifically
told otherwise. When acting in corporate films, you are dealing with people who are even further removed from the
entertainment world than ad agency executives. They live
and work in an extremely conservative environment, and
want to project that in their training films. Business suits are
the order of the day.

The two keys to auditioning for these projects are an ability
to successfully use "substitution," and the ability to create
interesting relationships out of thin air. Let's go back to the
sample script. Neither you nor I know what a "Pre-
Allocation System" is, but we can assume it is a term the

average company insider knows. So what you want to do is imbue the term with the same *sense* as something you are familiar with. For example you can comfortably use the term "complete tune-up" in a sentence, right? Well, try saying "Pre-Allocation System" with the same familiarity and intonations. Toss it off in the same manner. This is using substitution effectively. Try saying "BALCOM" with the same sense as "Department of Motor Vehicles." Get it?

As for relationships, always sin on the side of familiarity. We don't know much about Carl and Bob except that they work for the same company. Why not make them really good friends, poker buddies? That way, Bob can be a little embarrassed at having to call on his close friend for such a dry assignment. In the explanation about Pre-Allocation Systems, their friendship can justify a sense of shared secrecy. When Bob is asked if he worked on the system, he can smile knowingly at a secret that only he and Carl share before answering, "Sure. We all did." These moments give flesh to extremely barren material and endear you to the producers. You have to remember that corporate scripts are not usually written by trained screenwriters, but by corporate types. They don't know how to weave in characterization and relationship, only how to convey stark information. They don't understand the necessity for conflict in a scene. If you can bring this kind of writing to life, it makes them look good.

When auditioning, react a lot. Keep your head out of the script when the other character is talking. Listen to him. React. *Then* go to the script for the next line. Acting has almost nothing to do with words, but these scripts are almost nothing *but* words. Find ways to break up the speaking. By interacting with the other actor as much as possible, you'll also be letting the camera see you more.

HOW TO FIND THE JOBS

Industrial/educational films have many possible origins and myriad uses, so you have to be entrepreneurial if you want to tap into them. True, many are cast through regular channels, via talks between a casting director and an agent, but just as many are handled as in-house productions for major companies, and you'll never know about them if you don't dig.

A good place to start would be with a list of corporations with headquarters in your city. Get on the phone and ask for the education or training department. Once connected, identify yourself as an actor and ask if they produce training films. If they do, ask if they maintain photo files. Some will, some will not. Those that don't probably rely on the freelance director to find actors. Ask if they work with any particular directors a lot. Try to get names you can track down. Then, call the directors and ask if they maintain files.

Another good reference is one of the sourcebooks that are regularly used by the advertising industry. On the West Coast, the *411 Directory* is good, or the *REEL Directory* in San Francisco. In New York, *The Madison Avenue Handbook* fills the same need. Since ad agencies use these books, directors in search of work tend to advertise in them. Go down the list of directors and look for those that claim a specialty in industrial/educational/corporate films. Call them up and follow through with a photo in the mail and maybe a visit.

Corporate films that are cast in the offices of talent agents are a different kind of problem. Because of the agent's franchise agreement with the performers' unions, he cannot function as a casting director. That means he cannot call other agents for submissions. Instead, he can only call in his own actor-clients. If you are signed to such an agent, you'll probably get in anyway. If you are a free-lancing actor, accepting auditions from several different agents, it is not quite so automatic, and is a good argument for keeping in touch with agents on a regular basis. More on this in Chapter 11.

Once you have performed in an industrial film, it is a good idea to ask for a videotape copy of your work. Most employers will provide this, perhaps for the cost of blank tape. Excerpt your scenes, or at least the best ones, and put them on a demo reel that you can then show to other potential employers. When you call the corporations or directors, instead of simply asking if they accept photos, you can ask if they will look at your reel. That implies experience in the field, and should help open the doors.

Working in corporate films is an excellent, low-profile way to develop your camera technique, but an industrial demo reel won't be of much use when trying to land an agent, unless that agent does a lot of industrial work. He will be responsive to a commercial reel, or one with excerpts from films and TV shows, but an industrial reel is a very specific kind of thing. It provides currency only when dealing with people in that field.

THE FUTURE OF INDUSTRIAL FILMS

Technological advances are really shaking things up here, fueling explosive growth. The most recent development is the marriage of the personal computer to the video-disc player, creating something called interactive video. With interactive video, employee training can be done on a one-to-one basis, and studies indicate there is 50 percent higher retention than with regular corporate films.

The viewer puts a video disc into the machine, presses the start button, and a custom-made training film unfolds on the TV screen before him. At selected intervals, the action on screen stops, and the viewer is presented with multiple-choice questions. If he answers one way, that keys the machine to play scenario #1, and if he keys another, it goes to scenario #2. The interactive quality keeps the viewer on his toes, thus increasing retention. The word on the street is that this technology will one day be used for producing feature films with alternate endings. Science fiction comes to life.

9

Auditioning for the Stage

The years I spent in New York doing play after play Off-Off Broadway and even Off-Off-Off Broadway were at once thrilling and invaluable, and I think of them fondly. The stage is home, and no matter how deeply entrenched you may get in the more lucrative world of film and TV, there is always a comfortable feeling going home.

The stage is an *actor's* medium, in contrast to movies, which are generally considered a *director's* medium. This is where all actors are equal, where it is not considered bad form to play a small role in one production and a large one in the next. This is where you can take your best shot at playing Hamlet or Maggie the Cat. It is an arena in which the transaction between actor and audience is at its purest. No one is going to yell ''cut!'' if a scene isn't going right, and there is no such thing as a ''pick-up.'' A theater is a place where we get together to inspire one another, to feed our souls. I have to believe that, one day, it will be possible to make a decent living in this most fragile of art forms.

Michael Shurleff's *Audition* is the seminal text on the craft of auditioning for stage—if you don't already own a copy, you should. What Shurleff has to say about specific techniques an actor can use to propel himself into a cold reading is invaluable, and I have used much of his advice myself. What I want to do here, however, is talk about the differences between an audition for stage and those for the other media. In that regard, there is much to be said.

HOW STAGE PRODUCTIONS ARE CAST

In the theater, a paid casting director is a luxury that isn't always in the budget. You will rarely encounter them in Equity Waiver (non-paying) plays or in summer-stock companies, but they are usually present in regional theaters and on Broadway.

If a casting director is part of the production, he will function a lot like the casting director for a movie. That is, he will work closely with the director and will be intimately familiar with the play being mounted. He is also going to want to pre-screen you if he doesn't already know your work.

A pre-screen interview for stage offers you the opportunity to present prepared monologues. This is an excellent way for the casting director to get an idea of what you can do, and it gives you the advantage of being able to prepare in advance rather than having to read totally cold from sides. We'll take a close look at monologues and how to select them a little later in this section.

Stage auditions can be held almost anywhere, since they don't involve videotape. They might be on a stage or in a drafty rehearsal hall somewhere, but they will invariably be conducted in a location that allows you to move around during your audition, to be physical. This alone makes a stage audition radically different from reading in a cramped production office on a back lot.

Unless you are auditioning to replace a cast member in a long-running show, your audition will invariably be conducted by the actual director. Replacement roles are usually cast by producers and stage managers, since the director has moved on to other projects.

You will probably be reading with the stage manager instead of the casting director. If a casting director is part of the picture, his primary job involves finding the actors and bringing them in. During the readings, he is likely to be sitting next to the director, making notes of his own.

The director is firmly in charge at the auditions. He might ask the casting director for information on particular actors, and he may confer with the producers from time to time, but basically, casting is his domain. Everybody wants the director to be happy, and once he is hired, he is given wide latitude in casting decisions.

His right-hand person is the stage manager, whose job begins with these auditions and extends through the run of the show. When rehearsals start, the stage manager will keep a record of all blocking and light cues, will make sure props are in place before work begins each day, and will coordinate schedules. Once the play opens, he runs it while the director moves on to other projects. The stage manager has the responsibility of deciding when to hold a curtain, handling emergencies, and making sure the cast is all accounted for at the proper time. You might say he is a central control mechanism for the overall production, and he represents the director in his absence.

Reading with a stage manager is exactly like reading with a casting director except that, this being stage, he will get up on his feet and move around with you if the scene requires it. Like a casting director, he will not "play" the scene, but will give you lines, reading all of the parts except yours.

WHAT THE DIRECTOR IS LOOKING FOR

Stage productions enjoy the luxury of rehearsal, and that fact deeply colors what the director is looking for in the auditions. He knows that, once the cast is set, there will be a period of intense experimentation, an opportunity for all of the actors to explore their roles in collaboration with him. Therefore, he doesn't want to see a final performance at the audition. In fact, if he thinks he is seeing a final performance, a frozen performance, he likely will not cast you.

The image I am most fond of in this context is that of a race horse. The director knows there is going to be a race later on, but right now, he just wants to see you go around the track a couple of times. He wants to learn about your personality as well as your talent. He wants to see how physical you are, how agile, what kind of voice you have, how intelligent you are, how well you respond to adjustments, what kind of "chemistry" you have with him. In addition to casting actors for roles, he is forming a family that will have to work closely together for a concentrated time, so when he is auditioning you, he has part of his mind on the other members of the cast. This is in dramatic contrast to movies and TV, where actors come in, do their thing, and leave, having no real involvement with the rest of the cast or the director. A stage play is an ensemble effort, a piece of art that everybody contributes to. It starts taking shape the first day of rehearsal, but the final form is unknown until it gets in front of an audience. Even then, it continues to evolve.

As with any audition, you should know what your character wants in a scene, where the scene takes place, and what the relationship is between you and the other characters. But on stage, you also want to show your potential. For that, your choices can be dangerously bold. For example, play opposites—if a scene calls for an emotional outburst, try to find a way to contain it rather than giving in to it. Instead of yelling, use quiet intensity. If a line calls for anger, use irony instead. Use humor any place you can. Don't play the obvious choices, play against them. It really does not matter if your audition choices are not appropriate to the character because the director figures you will find the character before the show's opening. What you want to do is show off your moves, your style. You want the director to see as many of your strengths as possible.

HELPFUL HINTS

Following are some concrete suggestions for auditioning for the stage, some things to try and a few to avoid:

- Use the entire stage. If you have a reason to move, do so. Don't stay rooted to the spot. It is visually inter-

esting to see an actor turn his back on the auditors
and cross to the upstage wall. Just be sure the move is
motivated. Try sitting on the apron of the stage. Sit
down and lean against a wall. Remember that words
are just part of what is going into the director's brain.
What he is seeing is vitally important. Try to be visually interesting.

- Get the words off the script. It drives me crazy to
  watch an actor following along in his script while the
  stage manager is reading the other characters. *Listen*
  to what is being said to you. *React.* Then look in the
  script for the next line.

- Learn how to deal with physicality in auditions. Kissing scenes and fighting scenes lead actors right down
  the road to ruin. What you have to do is learn how to
  ''mark through'' extreme action. If a scene calls for a
  tender kiss, try a tender touch on the cheek instead. If
  it calls for a roundhouse right, try a gentle shove and
  allow the stage manager to recoil on his own. I have
  watched actors practically destroy stage managers,
  scratching and clawing and slugging. I've also seen
  actresses grab for crotches in necking situations. The
  rule of thumb is not to get entangled in any way at an
  audition. You can't deal with the stage manager, your
  lines, a script, and a fistfight all at the same time.

- Keep the script in your hand and refer to it from time
  to time, even if you have received a script in advance
  and have memorized the scene. If the director sees
  you playing without a script, he might think this is as
  good as you get, that this is a final performance.

- Learn the strength in keeping a distance between the
  stage manager and yourself. For some reason, actors
  just love to close in dramatically, to get right up in the
  stage manager's face. They will invariably do it in a fit
  of anger, as they rush threateningly toward their partner. Then you can see it flash through their brain that
  they somehow have to get *out* of the stage manager's
  face so they can continue the scene. Try looking at it

this way: rushing up in your partner's face is equivalent to an exclamation point, so use it sparingly. Anyway, it creates a far stronger visual image and increases tension to play from the opposite side of the stage than your partner.

MONOLOGUES

If you want to act on the stage, sooner or later you'll be asked to bring in those "contrasting monologues," so you might as well get them ready. This is a never-ending task because you'll always be updating them, always keeping an eye out for that special selection that shows you off to just the right advantage.

I've seen hundreds of actors present monologues, and I'm fascinated by the generally weak material selected. Too many actors confuse monologues with stand-up routines and cute stories. They come out on stage and muse about something with no particular motivation for the telling. We're not auditioning writers, remember. A good monologue selection is one that causes the actor to *do* something, and if it's physical, all the better.

Let's go back to that image of the actor as a race horse. If you want to show off your best form, you're not just going to stand there in the middle of the field and let them admire you, are you? No, you're going to jump some hurdles, strut a little, maybe hit a gallop. Right? Well, your monologue combination should show you off in the same way.

Usually, they ask for contrasting pieces, something classical and something contemporary. Except in Hollywood. Some theaters there have finally given up asking for classical selections in a movie town and satisfy themselves with contrasting contemporary selections. A sad commentary. You should presume, however, that they want classical and contemporary.

If you choose a dramatic classical selection, then your contemporary piece should be comedic. If one of them is physical, then the other should be still. *Contrast* them.

Where can you find these pieces? Anywhere! The entire

world of plays and literature is at your disposal. Here are some sample combinations and suggestions as to how to proceed.

A good classical selection for an actor would be from *The Tempest* by Shakespeare, Act II, Scene II. Trinculo, a very pampered court jester, is beside himself with worry over an approaching storm and is trying to find a place to hide. The set-up allows the actor to run all over the stage before cozying up to the smelly savage, Caliban. Very funny stuff, extremely physical.

A nice contrasting contemporary selection would be from *I Never Sang for My Father* by Robert Anderson. At the very end of Act II, Gene turns to the audience and talks about his final visit with his father, trying to express a love he has been unable to put into words. Poignant and still, a perfect accompaniment to *The Tempest*.

An actress might try the role of Dorine in *Tartuffe* by Molière as a classical selection. In Act II, Scene II, she takes Orgon to task for wanting to marry his daughter Mariane to the scheming Tartuffe. She is saucy, even sassy, and full of venom as she makes her case.

Then, as a contrast, turn to Act I of *The Woolgatherer* by William Mastrosimone. Rose, having invited an amorous truck driver to her apartment, suddenly surprises him by telling of a terrifying attack on the flamingos at the zoo. Obviously still upset by what she has seen, her descriptions are almost cinematic. Wonderful writing, even if the play is a bit strange, and a good counterpart to Dorine.

Molière is a fruitful source for actresses in search of monologue material, by the way, arguably better than Shakespeare. I have always felt that the men's roles in Shakespeare's plays are stronger than the women's. Molière cared about mistreatment of women and made it a recurrent theme. His women are full-blooded and active, frequently scheming, and almost always funny. And, of course, we now have Richard Wilbur's wonderful translations. Molière simply seems to offer fresher choices to me than dusting off Kate from *Taming of the Shrew* once again.

Another Molière play, *The Misanthrope*, has a juicy role in

Celimene, and the exchange with her friend Arsinoe in Act III, Scene V, is biting comedy at its best. They go at each other with claws bared, and Celimene's description of party gossip about Arsinoe is excellent monologue material.

A companion piece might be from *The Fox* by D.H. Lawrence, as adapted for the stage by Allan Miller. Act III, Scene II has Jill trying to warn her companion, Nellie, about the dangers of involvement with Henry. Jill is as earnest as Celimene is arch. Nice counterpoint.

Yet another possible combination for an actress would be Lady Anne's speech over Henry's casket in *Richard III*, Act I, Scene II, contrasted with *Division Street* by Steve Tesich. In Act I, Dinah tells her lawyer, Sal, how attracted she was to Chris, the counterculture leader of the Sixties. The material presents an actress with the opportunity to absolutely chew up the stage if she wants.

Prince Hal's scene with his father (King Henry) in Act III, Scene II of *Henry IV, Part I* is marvelous. Suddenly, the boy becomes a man and promises that the king will be proud of him yet. This is wonderful material for an actor, and it can be contrasted with something like Jonathan's stuttering speech in *Oh Dad, Poor Dad, Mamma's Hung You in the Closet and I'm Feelin' So Sad* by Arthur Kopit, in which Jonathan tells Rosalie about his telescope (Act I, Scene II).

Try not to use material that has been made into a popular movie. If you do, the director may compare whatever you do to a wonderful memory he has of the perfect production.

It's okay to take material from a novel instead of a play if you find something wonderful. They probably won't ask you where your material is from anyway, but if they do, just mention the book. Stay away from selections that are overused. Much of Neil Simon's work is a problem in this way, as is Tennessee Williams.

Think of your monologue combination as a little three-minute play, complete with a beginning, middle and end. Consider the overall package when deciding what to do and, just like a good play, build the tension. Pick material that has a clear action to play, something that can involve you immediately.

It doesn't matter if you combine a contemporary comedy selection with a classical dramatic selection, or a contemporary dramatic selection with a classical comedy selection. The important thing is that your choices contrast with each other. If you have writing talents, feel free to write your own contemporary piece.

You can rewrite, delete or otherwise alter material to fit your needs, even with Shakespeare. It would be sacrilege to change a word of Arthur Miller or O'Neill in an actual production, but anything goes in an audition.

You will find any number of "Guides to Monologues" on the market, little books in which some enterprising person has done a lot of leg work for you, excerpting monologues. By all means, refer to them for ideas, but remember this: every actor and his brother go through these same books, so the material is apt to be done a lot. Even more important, if you find something that you like, read the entire play! Do not simply memorize the selection out of the book. Learn something about the character. Be prepared to talk intelligently about your selection if the director wants you to. What would you do if, after putting up your piece, the director told you he had directed the play your selection was from? Would you be caught flat-footed?

An Audition Checklist

Be sure to ask your agent the following questions before any audition:

- If the audition is for a commercial, what is the product, and how will the spot air? It makes a difference whether you are up for a national spot or one that will run in metropolitan Albany. You may not want to do a fast-food commercial unless it is sure to air broadly, for example, because of the "conflict" category. And you may have personal objections to the product. Would you unilaterally accept any commercial for a laxative product? The time to make all of this clear is before the audition, not after. These are particularly important questions for those actors who are free-lancing with several different agents and not signed to an exclusive contract. The agents you free-lance with don't have a vested interest in your career; they don't really care what you do so long as they collect their 10 percent. It doesn't make them bad people, it only means that they might not volunteer the information you need. You have to ask.

- Is there a particular dress requirement for the audition? Is a business suit mandatory?

- If the audition is for film/TV/stage, will you be reading for the actual director or the casting director? Is this a pre-screen?

- Who is the director? If the audition is for a commercial, the agent won't always know this, but if it is film/TV/stage, he should. It is useful information because you might be familiar with other work by the same director. It could help you get a feel for his style.

- If you will be driving to the audition, are there any specific parking instructions? Will you be given a drive-on pass if the audition is on one of the studio lots? If you aren't certain about how to find the address, ask the agent for directions.

- If the audition is for film/TV/stage, is it possible to obtain a complete script rather than sides? If so, where can you pick it up, and when? If you can't get access to a complete script, would it be okay to sit in the casting director's outer office and read it? Remember, the better you know a script, the more intelligent will be your audition, particularly if your character has to interact with others in several scenes. If you are reading for a small part, just a few lines, you won't need to see a complete script.

Check off the following items that you will need to take to an audition:

- A photo and resume, neatly stapled together. Do this even if you have reason to believe the agent already sent a photo to the casting director.

- Materials with which to mark your script. A hi-lighter is handy.

- A breath freshener.

- Change for parking meters.

- A toothbrush, or at least a toothpick, if you are going to be eating between home and the audition. You don't want to be giving your all with a piece of celery stuck between your front teeth.

- A comb and/or hairbrush. Also, take something to pin your hair back if you need to.

- The notes you made when your agent first called with the audition.

- *After* the audition, as soon as you get out of the building, before you have time to forget, jot down the names of the people who saw your audition and specify their functions if you can. This information is invaluable at a callback, or if your agent asks what happened. Post it to your permanent files for future reference.

PART THREE

THE BUSINESS SIDE OF ACTING

10

Managing Your Acting Career

If you get in your car and don't have any place to go, you are just going to drive around. The chief executive of every single Fortune 500 company understands this, and that is why their firms operate on five-year plans and long-term projections. Why should the business of acting be any different? Not only is this a business like any other, it is a particularly competitive one, one in which the supply of actors far outstrips the available jobs. Seeking employment as an actor is a bit like selling snowcones in the Antarctic.

Over half the people who come into acting as a career get out within three years, so they say. I know many talented actors who simply gave up and walked away because they couldn't stomach the business side of the business. On the other hand, I've known more than a few who are arguably lacking in the talent department but who are just good salesmen—and they prosper. Nobody said it was fair.

There is definitely a luck factor to an actor's career. It is always possible to stumble into that one-time role that is the perfect showcase, and it is possible to find yourself sitting next to the Head of Talent for NBC the next time you are on jury duty. Sure, it's always possible to get hit by a car if you hang around in the street long enough. But that is certainly not a dependable way to get from point A to point B. A wise actor will not depend on luck, but will run his career as the business it is.

Let's draw an analogy. Suppose you were going into business selling refrigerators. What would you do? Would you just announce to your mom and dad and neighbors that you are in the refrigerator business and then wait for the phone to ring with orders? Of course not. What you would do is make a business plan. You would make sure you have proper office space, a good record-keeping system, an advertising campaign, a sales staff of some kind, and some long-range projections. On the day you open your doors for business, you would have some idea of the number of refrigerators you hope to sell next year.

Now, let's apply the same standard to acting.

First of all, you need a good product. Your refrigerator has to work. For the actor, that means you have to develop your craft, to stay in training. It means you have to watch your weight if that's a problem for you, and to resist the urge to start sporting green spiked hair. You want your product to be acceptable to middle America.

You need proper office space. If you were selling refrigerators, you'd probably rent a storefront and display your goods in the window. You'd probably have a desk somewhere in the back of the store. Well, an actor doesn't need a storefront, but he does need a desk area, some place at home that is specifically set aside for business affairs. And he needs to make sure that he tends to business in that space every single business day.

You need a record-keeping system. Otherwise, how are you going to keep track of what you are doing? For actors, this can be a simple file card system. I use one divided into categories headed "Agents," "Casting Directors," "TV," "Stage," "Current Projects," etc. In each category, I have a 3 x 5 card for each person I want to stay in touch with or whom I want to remember. Actors meet an incredible number of directors, casting directors, and others—after a couple of years, the names and faces start to blur. A file card system makes it possible to run a history on each person. That way, when you get an audition, you can check your card for an update on the people you'll be seeing. I even include information like whether a person is fat or skinny, a smoker or not, loud or not, cerebral or not, funny or not. Your record-keeping system should also have some way of tracking your own residual payments from commercials and such. Get a ledger book and ask someone at the union to show you how to log in payments when you start getting them. That way, at year end, you'll be able to compare your figures against the W-2s you'll get. This system will also help you keep track of which W-2s are still outstanding. It isn't uncommon for actors to have as many as twenty different employers in the course of a year.

You need an advertising campaign. For the actor, this means you have to have good photos, picture postcards, promotional flyers from time to time, notices in trade publications, and anything else that can announce what you have for sale. In addition, you would probably employ some commissioned salesmen to sell your refrigerators. Actors' commissioned salesmen are called talent agents, and you should make it your business to work with good ones. Even when you have them, however, never forget that this is *your* career we are talking about, and you never should give control of your career over to anyone else. If you were selling those refrigerators, you wouldn't let the salesmen out front run your business, would you? It is your responsibility to keep up with industry trends, to read trade publications like *Hollywood Reporter, Back Stage, Daily Variety, American Theatre Magazine, Dramalogue,* maybe even the Sunday *New York Times.* You have to find out what is happening in the marketplace and then initiate activity. Don't just sit there waiting for the phone call from your agents.

You need long-range projections. What do you want to be doing five years from now? Movies? Television? Commercials? A combination? How much money do you want to be making? If you want to make it happen, you should have a plan. What you need to do is work backward, starting five years from now. The reasoning goes this way: in order to be where I want to be five years from now, where do I have to be four years from now? In order to be where I want to be four years from now, where do I have to be three years from now? Two years? One year? Six months from now? One month from now? If I want to be where I should be one week from now, what should I be doing today to get me there?

By applying business standards to the acting profession, you will avoid the extreme emotional highs and lows. If you sold a refrigerator, that would be good news, but it wouldn't be occasion to close up shop and vacation in the Bahamas for a month. It would be another wonderful sale, and would hopefully lead to others. By the same token, if your refrigerators were not selling, if you hit a dry spell (and, take it from me, you will), you would know that an adjustment to your game plan was necessary. Maybe you would devise a new promotional drive, do a special mailing, get new pictures made. The thing you wouldn't do is go spinning into abject depression because of the lack of sales. Your commitment to your profession would be based on firmer ground.

Several years ago, the National Sales Executive Association released some figures that I think have specific relevance for actors. The figures were based on just such activities as selling refrigerators.

- 80 percent of all sales in the country are made after the fifth call on the same prospect.

- 48 percent of all salesmen make one call and cross the prospect off.

- 25 percent quit after the second call.

- 12 percent call three times and quit.

- 10 percent keep calling.

- On a national average, 10 percent of all salesmen make 80 percent of the sales.

To me, these figures speak of the value of long-term commitment and organized persistence, and I can think of nothing more important for the actor to consider. Try thinking of it this way: the business of acting is the search for employment. The acting is the fun part. Keep your eye on the target, and you have a decent chance of hitting it.

11

Finding and Keeping an Agent

An agent is an actor's broker, his representative in the marketplace. If you want to make money from acting, you have to have at least one, maybe two or three, and the quest for this representation can be a source of career-long anxiety. An agent is technically employed by an actor to provide a service; that's why the IRS says that his commissions are deductible on your taxes. That fact would suggest that you could therefore simply go out and hire one, but in the real world it's not as easy as that. The catch-22 is that the easiest agents to secure are frequently the lowest ones on the totem pole. The really excellent agencies, the ones whose clients are seen for all the best work, seem to always have a full client list, not needing new people; anyway, they are too busy to set up general interviews. I can think of very few actors who have not, at one time or another, felt like banging their heads against a wall over this issue.

Good news: you can get good representation if you want to, and if you are willing to persist with the effort. The trick is to be organized and smart about the pursuit, to look at the big picture.

HOW AGENTS WORK

Outside of New York and Los Angeles, franchised agencies are universally "full service." That means they represent performers for theatrical work as well as commercials, and they may handle children as well as adults. They may even have fashion modeling and print departments. In Hollywood, most agencies specialize either in theatrical (film/TV/stage) or commercial representation, and a performer who wants to work in both arenas has to have two different agents. In New York, there are both specialty and full-service agencies. How do you know if an agency is full-service or not? Check its franchises. The list provided by SAG gives an indication of an agency's specialties, if any.

It is very important that you restrict your search for an agent to only those that are franchised by the performers' unions. They have signed agreements with SAG, AFTRA, and AEA which allow them to represent union performers in exchange for abiding by fairly extensive rules and regulations set down by the unions to protect performers. They also agree not to take more than 10 percent commission on an actor's earnings. Any person who is seriously interested in acting as a career would be a fool to sign up with a non-franchised agent for the simple reason that the unions have a hammerlock on the business.

In Los Angeles, there are over 200 franchised agents and, in New York, a bit over half that. There are franchised agents in virtually every major city, including San Francisco, Detroit, Dallas, and Atlanta. No matter where you live, you should have access to one or more.

Before you start pursuing them, you should consider the distinctions between commercial and theatrical agents because this will color your approach. A commercial agent is mightily influenced by physical type and a winning personality. If you don't have an extensive acting background, it's not the end of the world from their perspective. As we've already seen, many non-actors do get cast in commercials. Therefore, it's not unusual for a commercial agent, if smitten with a non-actor, to go ahead and represent him and merely suggest that he take a commercial auditioning workshop. A theatrical agent, on the other hand, has to know that you can actually act. Yes, he is influenced by type, but he can't be sending non-actors to stage or movie auditions, so he is not going to represent you unless he is satisfied that you can deliver the goods.

A theatrical agency will represent far fewer actors than will a commercial agency, probably fifty on average as opposed to five hundred on average in the major markets, so this kind of representation is more difficult to obtain. Many performers who have done a lot of commercials still can't seem to get a good theatrical agent.

Full-service agencies vary dramatically in size, ranging from a company with only one or two agents to huge operations with several agents handling commercials and several more handling theatrical, all under the same roof. If you live outside of New York and Los Angeles, the odds are that the full-service agencies you pursue will employ fewer agents and will earn most of their commissions from commercials, not theatrical. This is important to remember because, though these agents will have an eye on your acting credentials, they have their bank book geared to commercials. The fastest way to representation in those companies is to fit into their commercial criteria. More on that later.

SETTING UP AN INTERVIEW

No matter where you live, there is a standard procedure suggested for approaching agents. It is entirely possible, even likely, that this effort will not get you over the wall of the fortress the first time, and you may have to regroup and try again. Primarily, this is due to the huge volume of aspiring actors trying to gain entrance, and you shouldn't let it bother you.

First, make sure you have a good 8 x 10 photo (see ''Theatrical Photos and Resumes''). Obtain the current list of franchised agents from Screen Actors Guild. If you live in L.A. or New York, you might also want to visit a theatrical book store and purchase one of the publications that include names of specific agents within the agencies and editorial comment about agency specialties. This way, you can cut down the list to a nice neat 30 or so that could be considered prime candidates. Send your photo and resume (if you have one) to as many agents as you want simultaneously. You don't have to wait for a response from one before approaching another. Be sure to send the material to specific people, not simply to agencies; it is okay to address agents by their first names.

If no one has called you within a week or so, you should call the agency. When the receptionist answers, ask to speak to the person you sent the photo to. If she asks what you want with him, tell her it is regarding representation, and that you've already sent a photo and resume. This is how she is almost guaranteed to respond: "We don't represent people who aren't in the union," or "We already have too many actors of your type," or "We look at photos every third Friday, and if there is interest, we'll be in touch," or "We are too busy at the present time to hold interviews—try again in a few months." It all adds up to the infamous "Don't call us, we'll call you."

All right, now what? You've done all of the right things and have come up empty-handed. It's time to regroup. You'll have to try an alternative approach.

THE SECOND APPROACH

All you can really be certain of at this point is that you don't have an interview. You can't presume that anyone has, in fact, looked at your photo unless you spoke directly to the agent you sent it to. It might still be sitting on a desk with two hundred others, still in unopened envelopes. Agents can receive as many as twenty-five pictures a day, and it is entirely possible they simply have not gotten to you yet. Or it may have been tossed in the trash. I have watched my own agents go through the daily incoming photos, and it is a sobering experience. They will open an envelope, pull out the picture, glance at it for maybe five or ten seconds, and make a snap decision, either putting it in a "to be called" stack or in the trash. It is a knee-jerk response to the overwhelming volume of aspiring actors.

If three weeks go by and you still haven't heard anything, you can conclude that you made it to the trash can and start trying to figure out why. A theatrical agent probably passed on you because you either lack sufficient acting background, or are too much like his other clients, physically. Remember, he is only going to represent a few actors, and he doesn't want too much duplication on his client list. A commercial agent probably passed on you because you do not fit into a definable type category, or you fall into the most populated one. I recently had a chat with one of Hollywood's busiest commercial casting directors, and asked her to break down the basic type categories of actors, knowing these would be her criteria when talking to agents. Here is her list:

1. Kids, 4 to 6, 7 to 10, and 10 to 12 years old.

2. Teenagers, 13 to 17.

3. College types, 18 to 22. Preppy, bright.

4. Yuppies, 25 to 39. These are professional, managerial, or administrative people who live in a metropolitan area. Male and female.

5. Nice Midwestern moms and dads, 28 to 32.

6. Jocks, 26 to 36. Outdoorsy guys, beer drinkers.

7. Spokesmen and -women, 35 to 45. Good-looking, solid, able to handle a lot of dialogue.

8. Beautiful people, 18 to 25. Models fall into this category.

9. Blue-collar character men, 28 to 48.

10. Character, comedic men and women, 35 to 50.

11. Handsome, late-middle-aged men and women. Includes doctors, lawyers, chairmen of the board, executives.

12. Ethnic types, Asian and Hispanic, all ages.

13. Grandma and Grandpa.

Notice that there isn't a category for regular-looking people in the 18-to-27 age group. Isn't that interesting? It surely
can't be because there aren't any people in that group, because it is the most populous of all. What it means is that
even if you fall in this group, you *still* must fit into a type
category as defined by the casting directors and agents.

"But I don't want to be typed," you may protest. "I'm an
actor and can play all kinds of different roles!" Before you
get too worked up over this, put yourself back in the agent's
seat for a minute as he is going through that stack of photos.
He is looking at prospective new clients, and he is balancing
what he sees against a mental checklist of types exactly like
the one above. If he can't categorize you immediately, he will
surely pass on you.

Maybe the picture you sent in is *too* middle-of-the-road.
What would happen if you wore glasses? If you wore a
business suit instead of a sweater/shirt combo? How about if
you got a haircut? Went from blonde to brunette? Got rid of
the toupee? Shaved your mustache? Is your existing picture
sending a mixed message? If you are a woman over thirty,
and you are still wearing hair down to your waist, that is a
mixed message. Hair that long is for young girls.

For a second approach, you might want to try to fudge
yourself into one of the type categories and have new photos
taken. Maybe you want a down-the-middle headshot in addition to a couple of shots that firmly categorize you. It's
perfectly all right to send more than one picture in the
packet. (I would advise against a composite at this point,
however. See "Theatrical Photos and Resumes.")

Go ahead and send your new pictures to the same group
you hit the first time, and see what happens. Don't worry
that they will remember your first submission. They won't.
Between then and now, they've seen another eight thousand
pictures, and you didn't make that much of an impression
the first time around anyway.

If there is no response within a week, start calling just as
before. Only this time, try calling at different times of the day
than you did last time. Receptionists work a fairly structured
schedule, so try calling early in the morning or after five. You
might luck out and get one of the agents on the phone.

Remember, keep notes on your 3 x 5 cards of each effort to make contact.

Repackaging yourself like this probably won't help with theatrical agents. With them, you might try some of the tactics suggested below.

IF YOU STILL CAN'T GET THROUGH

Still can't get through? Okay, try this: send a short, hand-written note to the agents. Enclose a resume, but instead of an 8 x 10 photo, use a picture postcard (see "Theatrical Photos and Resumes"). Send it all in a letter-size envelope. That way, when the morning mail arrives, your letter will go into a different stack than the usual twenty 8 x 10 envelopes. You can be pretty certain that the agent will read this one. Your note should say something like: "Dear Bob: I sent my photo and resume in a while back, but I got stopped by your agency moat. Congratulations on having the most efficient staff in town. Still, I want to meet you. You are a top agent, and I think we might work well together. How about a chat?"

If he doesn't respond to that, you are dealing with a person who is hard-core. Try sending a telegram. Be cute and brief. If that doesn't work, start all over again, this time pursuing another agent within the agency. You can always try simply dropping by the agency, but you will probably meet the same receptionist you've been talking to on the phone. Dropping by is more of a New York phenomena because "making rounds" is a way of life there; people don't do that in Hollywood very much.

No matter how hard an agent may be to reach, it can be done. I have never in nineteen years seen anybody not get through if he really wanted to and was persistent. The acting business is not like a department store—there isn't a person-nel director who automatically interviews anybody who sends in an application.

Keep an eye peeled for new agencies. When a talent agency opens its doors for business, the owners usually announce the fact to the trade via ads in industry publications like *Back Stage* and *Variety*. This is absolutely the best time to go after them. You know for certain that they don't have a client list yet and have to build one, so they'll be more open to seeing new people. Just be sure that the new agencies you pursue are staffed by experienced agents rather than people who are making an initial foray into agenting. You don't want to sign up with someone who has been selling Fords and wants to give actors a whirl. You need an agent who has established contacts with the casting directors.

THE INTERVIEW

Congratulations! You got the interview. Now what? It was hard to get, and you don't want to waste it. Here's what you can expect to happen when you get to the agency: if your interview is with a full-service or commercial agency, the agent will chat with you briefly, look at your resume or discuss your lack of one, and he might give you some commercial copy to read. Then, he may introduce you to his associates. Finally, he'll tell you that he and those associates will pow-wow and will let you know one way or the other in a day or two. In rare instances, he'll give a thumbs up or down right there on the spot.

An interview with a theatrical agent will also consist of a chat and, if he doesn't know your work, maybe the opportunity to do your monologues in the office. Introductions all around, and they will let you know in a day or two.

Before setting out for the interview, be sure you are dressed to fit your type category and that you look like your picture. Also, remember that an interview of this sort has the same dynamic as a commercial audition: high energy, positive sense of life.

During the interview, keep these points in mind:

- If the agent asks you to read copy for him, talk to him as if he were the camera. Play right to him as if he is a scene partner. A few agents might tell you not to do this because it makes them uncomfortable. Okay, then talk to something inanimate near their heads.

- Remember that everybody wants a winner. You want to give the impression that you will work with or without him, but you don't want to be cocky or arrogant about it. If you must, play mental tricks on yourself. Pretend you already have four commercials on the air or something, and assume that dynamic. The important thing is that you absolutely do not want to be dealing with the agent in a deferential way. He is your equal!

- Try to anticipate the trickiest questions so you can have positive answers for them. For example, "What have you done?" is a stopper for a lot of beginning actors. If you are inexperienced, it is easy to get defensive about it. (My favorite answer was given by a New York friend. When a casting director asked him that, he said, "Why? Do you smell something?" I wouldn't go that far.) A good answer might be that you've been taking classes and auditioning for Equity Waiver shows, that you've been really busy. Don't just sit there and look like a waif. Don't let them think that your main activity for the past six months has been trying to meet agents.

- If you are a non-actor, one of the most important things you can communicate to the agent is how serious you are about acting. Don't bring the subject up but, if he asks about your day job, tell him there is zero problem getting off to go to auditions, that your major interest in life is acting, and that you have structured your schedule to allow for that priority. Do not waffle on this point! I saw one new actress cost herself an agent because she insisted on discussing her day job with him. The agent doesn't care if you are a brain surgeon and the President is one of your patients. He only wants to know if he can count on you to arrive on time for the Crest Toothpaste commercial.

If your interview is with a theatrical agency, there will be a different dynamic. You and the agent will chat, but you don't have to treat the meeting like a commercial audition. It is okay to kick back a bit. Hopefully, the agent will already know your work because he saw you in a play or student film. If he doesn't, you may get the opportunity to do your monologues in the office. He is not apt to spring this on you by surprise, though. When your appointment is first set, the receptionist will tell you if they expect you to perform in the office. Since a monologue can only tell part of the story, an agent will sometimes ask you to put up a scene instead and will schedule a second appointment time for that. If you run into that situation, keep these points in mind: (1) This is your audition, not your scene partner's. If you can, find a scene that is equally balanced, but at the very least, you should play the showier role. (2) All of the rules that apply to selecting stage monologue material apply here. Avoid plays that are too familiar or that have been made into a well-known movie. (3) The scene should be contemporary instead of classical, and should not be more than three or four minutes long. (4) If you have reason to believe that the agency in question does more television work than movie work, choose a comedic scene. If the agency is stage-oriented or does a lot of movies, you can get away with drama. After all of the meetings and/or office auditions are over, the agent will let you know whether or not the agency wants to represent you in a day or two.

EXCLUSIVITY VERSUS FREE-LANCE REPRESENTATION

During the years I lived and worked in New York, I free-lanced. That is, I did not sign a contract with a single agent, preferring to accept auditions and jobs from any agent who would call me. I "made rounds" of the agencies, staying in touch with several on an almost daily basis. After moving to Hollywood, I signed exclusive contracts with specialty agencies, one for commercials and one for theatrical, because that is what the unions require in that city. Today, I even have a third agent, this one for voice work. In my opinion, it really doesn't matter if you are signed for exclusive representation just as long as you are getting auditions and work. You do whatever the marketplace demands, and there are arguments pro and con regarding exclusivity.

Pro: If you sign exclusively with an agent, he will take more of an interest in your career than he would if you were a free-lance client. Because you are signed exclusively, he will try harder to find you work.

Con: By signing exclusively with an agent, you are giving away a bit of your autonomy. You can't play agents off against each other, making each one of them believe that the others think you are hot stuff. If you are signed exclusively, you may have to compete within your own agency for spots at the audition, especially if the agent has several actors in your type category under contract.

Personally, I like the freedom of free-lancing, but I wouldn't stand in fire to defend it. For one thing, theatrical work is much harder to find if you are free-lancing than if you are signed. For another, even if you sign exclusive contracts, they are really written to protect the actor. If you don't make at least $2,000 in a ninety-day period, you can break them anyway. If you are making more than that, why would you want to break it?

A problem might arise if you live in a city where all the agencies are small full-service companies, and an agent from one of them wants to sign you. If he is very strong commercially, but weak theatrically, it could be a bad move to sign across-the-board. On the other hand, he might not take you at all unless you sign across-the-board. If confronted with such a situation, and if I was certain that I was dealing with one of the better agents in town, I would probably sign even if I was opposed to it in principle. I'd give it a year and see what happens. If it works, terrific; if not, I can always move on.

CHANGING AGENTS

There are a lot of reasons for changing agents. Maybe your hottest agent at the agency has left for another agency. Maybe you haven't had an audition in six months. Maybe you just don't have good chemistry with your agent. There is no easy way to do it, but everybody understands that it is done. Nothing personal. Be friendly, and don't burn any bridges. The day may come when you and the agent will work together again. I strongly advise you not to leave in a huff.

Also, don't leave one agent before finding another. It is accepted practice to be interviewing with other agents if you are not getting work, and you don't need to be defensive about it. It is unlikely that the agents you are seeing will call your current agent and tell on you.

Sometimes, it is necessary to change agents in order to get better roles. In Hollywood, some agents specialize in the smaller ''day player'' roles, and some work on leads and contract parts. If you have worked like a bandit at the day roles, one of the other agents might get interested in you. You'd wind up with fewer auditions, but for better stuff. Mind you, changing agents for this reason is guaranteed to irritate the agent you are leaving if he knows why you are going, so my advice is not to spell it out.

SOME PARTING THOUGHTS ON FINDING AND KEEPING AN AGENT

When you are pursuing agents, be nice to the receptionists. They are doing the best they can. Their's must be one of the most awful jobs in the entire world. Nobody in his right mind could *like* fighting off actors.

The fastest way to meet any agent is via personal introduction. He might see you on the recommendation of a current actor-client; he will always see you on the advice of a working casting director.

Never use trickery to gain an interview. I know one guy, a lawyer who was trying to break into acting, who sent agents subpoenas. Bad move. Another fellow identified himself to the receptionist as a former college buddy of the agent. He got through all right, but he just made the agent mad. Also, avoid trying anything risqué or in bad taste. Be inventive, by all means, but keep in mind that you are going to have to live with whatever you do. Vulgarity is a bad idea. Don't be like the actor who sent a female agent one silk stocking and a note explaining she could have the other one in exchange for an interview.

12

Theatrical Photos and Resumes

A theatrical photo is nothing like the shot you had taken in your senior year of high school; a theatrical resume bears little resemblance to the type used in the civilian world. These two elements will be the tools of your trade, and because you'll be sending them to agents and casting directors, it is crucial that both your photo and your resume be prepared just right.

THEATRICAL PHOTOS

"Fish got to swim, birds got to fly" . . . and actors got to have photos. I suppose that is why I have seen more money wasted in this area than in any other.

The mistakes fall into three categories: (1) bad photographer, (2) good photos that don't look like the person, and (3) bad reproduction.

The first thing to understand is that a theatrical photo is not like the picture of you sitting on the mantel at home. Stay away from neighborhood portrait studios and hide from Uncle Howie and his Minolta. You want to make certain that you get your pictures taken only by knowledgeable theater professionals.

The best way to find a good photographer is to ask other actors who they go to. Also, you can conduct your own little telephone poll of franchised agents in your city, asking each who they recommend to their clients. You'll start hearing the same names pop up again and again. Make some appointments with the photographers so you can drop by to chat. Look at their work. You should have a gut feeling about whether you are in the right place or not. Trust it. If the photographer seems to be intimidating to you, or if you think he is charging too much, move along. If you aren't comfortable with him, you will not get a good session.

The Theatrical Headshot

At minimum, you need one excellent headshot, a picture that looks exactly like you. An actress recently gave me a picture for feedback and, to tell the truth, if she hadn't been standing right there in front of me, I wouldn't have known she was the person in the shot. In life, she wore glasses and was roughly fifteen pounds overweight. Her complexion was freckly, and her hair was flaming red. The photo, on the other hand, was shot so that her hair appeared brunette; she wasn't wearing the glasses, was wearing too much eye makeup and evidently had the session before she gained the weight. Also, the girl in the picture was coming on like some kind of French movie, and the strongest quality of the real-life subject was an energetic, child-like innocence.

Not only was this actress walking around with a picture that was no good, she was actually in danger of making influential people angry. If someone looked at that shot and called the actress in for an interview, he would not be happy if someone else walked in. She would have been in trouble before even shaking hands.

Maybe the problem comes from the mistaken perception that professional theatrical pictures should be glamorous, should somehow fit a glamorous industry. Maybe every aspiring actress sees herself as a budding Marilyn Monroe, and every actor as Marlon Brando. I only know that I see a lot of pictures that don't look like the people who posed for them, and there is no question that such pictures are a bad mistake.

A good headshot is one that is shot on black-and-white film, preferably Plus-X or slower, with ample lighting. There shouldn't be a lot of shadows. Most important, the essential personality trait of the subject should be evident in the photo. In other words, we want to be looking at a picture of who the actor is right now, not who he would like to be, or who he can make himself up to be in a crunch.

It doesn't make any difference whether the picture is taken outdoors or in a studio. Many photographers prefer to work in a studio because it gives them more control, and that is a perfectly good reason. The picture I use now was shot inside, but the one I recently stopped using was shot outside.

As for what to wear, take your cue from commercials if the photo will be used for that purpose, or if you are trying to land a full-service agent. Stay with muted colors, no turtle-necks, spare jewelry. A jacket and tie is okay for men, but it is limiting. I favor a simple, open-neck sport shirt. The idea is to convey a sense of happy energy, confidence. If your picture is going to be used for purely theatrical purposes, the dress doesn't matter as much as the attitude. You don't need to stress animation so much in a theatrical shot. When a casting director looks at it, a good theatrical photo should convey the message: ''I know what I'm doing, and I like who I am; you know what you are doing. Let's get together and work on a project.'' Don't wear anything that is too sexy, low-cut, or otherwise revealing.

Whether your photo is for commercial or theatrical pur-poses, be warned against making your hair the star of the picture if you happen to own a gorgeous mane. They are not casting hair.

Makeup artists are an optional matter. Some photogra-phers include the services of one in their basic fee, and that's okay. I've personally never needed one, but then most men are going to wear only a pancake base and no eye makeup at all. Women might feel better if there is someone there to keep an eye on their hair and to make sure their forehead isn't shining. The only problem is the possibility that a makeup artist can make the actor look *too* perfect. It's not wonderful to have absolutely every hair in place.It doesn't look natural. (That's what is wrong with the picture your mom has on the mantel.)

Be very careful when touching up your photo. It is one thing to airbrush out a pimple that would go away in a day or two by itself, and it's quite another to cause a scar to disappear. Again, you need to look *exactly* like your photo. No wishful thinking. Don't be airbrushing out your wonderful age wrinkles. They look good, are a sign of experience. Leave them alone.

Composites

The typical composite used only for commercial purposes involves a single headshot on one side and four or five situational shots on the other side of the sheet. The idea is that a composite allows you to show an ad agency a lot of different roles you might want to play.

I don't believe you need a composite in order to get work. I didn't use one in New York, and it never hurt me. On the other hand, I have used one off and on in Hollywood, at the suggestion of various agents, and I haven't seen a significant increase in jobs. Mainly, they are expensive. However, if the agents in your city insist on them, go ahead and get one made.

If you do have a composite done, each situational shot should show a different way you can be cast in commercials. You might want a picture of you as a school teacher, another of you as an airline hostess, and another of you digging in the rose garden at home. They should be situational rather than presentational. The school teacher should be drying a child's tear, the airline hostess should be fluffing a pillow, that kind of thing. For some reason, many photographers do not give good guidance in this area. I've seen many composites where the actor is merely posed wearing different clothes in each shot, but not involved in any activity, and they look very stilted. Remember, too, that the picture should feature you, not a product. You don't want to be photographed standing there grinning over a can of Coke. It would be better to be pouring the coke for a friend. Get it?

Be inventive when choosing composite shots. A tele-phone-repair*woman* climbing up a telephone pole is a wonderful shot because it surprises. A man taking a casserole out of the oven works for the same reason. I saw a clever composite shot the other day in which a fellow had trapped a butterfly on his head with a net. Try to show some style with your pictures. I've seen actors also use the composite format for very original promotional purposes. One fellow has his headshot on the front and a picture of the back of his head on the back. Another has his baby pictures on the back. These things are fun, but I would use them as an addendum, not as your mainstay composite.

In New York and Hollywood, color shots will label you as a beginner, so don't use them. They are expensive to shoot and reproduce, and they won't get you any more work. Models use color shots in their portfolios, but actors don't need them. In some of the smaller cities, there are a few agents who like color shots, but if you head for the majors, switch to black-and-white fast.

What To Spend On Photos

How much to spend varies a lot with where you live, but generally, you can expect to pay a photographer between $125 and $200 for a session in which he takes one or two roles of film, and you get a headshot. A composite session can cost anywhere from $425 all the way up to $700 or so. It depends on how many locations are involved, how many rolls of film, how much time.

After your session, the photographer will give you contact sheets, unenlarged copies of the developed film. You will pick the shots you want enlarged to 8 x 10, and after the photographer gets those to you, you'll face the expense of having your photos reproduced. Composites are usually done with a lithographic process on a special paper, and it will cost you around $200, from start to finish, to get five hundred copies.

Regular headshots are generally reproduced at photo labs on glossy or pearl finish paper, but lithography is acceptable. You can figure it will cost you in the neighborhood of $100 to walk away with your first hundred copies. After that, the price drops because they don't have to keep making new negatives.

Reproduction can be a major problem because the duplicates can come out too contrasty. Your duplicates are never going to look as good as your original, so you should ask to see a proof before the lab proceeds to run off hundreds of them. If you don't, the lab will expect you to trust, and pay for, its judgment.

Postcards

Postcards are worth their weight in platinum. When you get your headshot or composite run off, order up some postcards at the same time. Most photo labs have desktop display books so you can examine the different possible formats. The one I favor most is a simple 4 x 6 card with a full headshot on one side and nothing at all on the other.

You can get postcards any size you want, but the reason I like 4 x 6 is that it will fit into a letter-size envelope. That way, you can use them for reaching hard-to-get-to people, like agents. You can zip right past that stack of 8 x 10s on the receptionist's desk if you use letter-size envelopes.

Once you have the postcards in your hot little hands, you should develop the practice of sending one to everybody you want to stay in touch with—every three or four weeks. It doesn't matter what you write on them. These are not "the weather's nice, wish you were here" postcards. Just write "Hiya" if you want. The point is to hit people like casting directors with your face again and again, until they finally remember who you are. These are a simply wonderful investment, and I can directly trace many jobs to their use.

THEATRICAL RESUMES

The theatrical resume is an actor's calling card, a form of introduction, something we run off by the hundreds and attach to our photos. It is not the kind of formal submission you might make to the personnel department of a Fortune 500 company.

Only theatrically relevant information should be on it. The fact that you hold a law degree or a Ph.D. in astrophysics is impressive but is not theatrically important. It means much more to a casting director or an agent that you studied for six months with Stella Adler or Sanford Meisner than it does that you once received the Silver Cross for bravery. They want to know what actual experience you have had performing and whom you have studied with, and that's about it.

The format of the resume itself—whether to put your stage credits or film credits at the top—depends on where you live. In New York, the first way is correct; in Hollywood, the second. In cities like Dallas and San Francisco, I would put stage credits on top, but that is a personal opinion. I am including two resumes from one of my bicoastal friends, one he uses in L.A. (page 131) and the other in New York (page 132). Same information, arranged differently.

Here are some helpful tips for creating your resume:

- Don't lie about your credits. It will only come back to haunt you.

- Don't inflate what you did. If you worked as an extra on a movie, don't try to make it look like you had a speaking part.

- Never, ever put extra work on a resume.

- Don't put the dates of productions next to the credits. It only makes the person reading the resume start focusing on how old you are, or it gets them wondering why there aren't more recent dates on there.

- Note that the sample resumes I have included do not list the actor's specific roles on TV and film. Instead, he cites billing.

- When you have your resumes run off at the printer, have them cut to 8 x 10 so they fit the size of your photo without overlapping.

JONATHAN SLAFF

AEA - SAG - AFTRA
Ht.: 5'11''   Wt: 165   Eyes: Blue
Hair: Brown   Voice: Baritone

FILMS	Beer	Orion (Bob Chartoff, Prod.)
	Zelig	Woody Allen, Dir.
	So Fine	Warner (Andrew Bergman, Dir.)

TELEVISION	All My Children	ABC
	Something Smells Sushi (pilot)	Huh—Choo Prod., NY
	The Executive Crunch (syndicated)	Cinetudes, NY
	Thomas Eakins (PBS)	Spofford Films, NY

NEW YORK	Die Kleine Esther	Elizabeth Swados, Dir.
THEATRE	The Men's Group	ELT @ Lincoln Center
	Imag. Coming Dead	Theatre for the New City
	Atonements	'' ''
	Marathon '33	Lion Theatre
	End as a Man	''

SUMMER	Make a Million	Kenley Players
STOCK	Heaven Can Wait	''
	The Merry Widow	''
	Kismet	''

| INDUSTRIAL | Matthew Bender Company |
| FILMS | (awards: Houston Int'l Film Fest., Industrial Film Fest.) |

COMMERCIALS   Reel available upon request.

TRAINING	Acting: Wynn Handman, Bob McAndrew, Stella Adler, Jack Waltzer
	Musical Theatre: David Craig, Albert Hague
	Singing: Harry Garland
	Stage Combat: Richard Coyne
	Dance: Jerri Lines, Kathy Burke

SPECIAL	Serious & Comedic Hand-to-Hand Combat, FLUENT GERMAN, Swimming,
SKILLS	Military Drill & Manual of Arms, Horseback Riding, Skiing,
	Motorcycle & Truck Driving, Tennis, Golf, CPR, Fly & Surf
	Casting.

| EDUCATION | BA Yale (history) |
| | MBA Columbia |

- Attach your resume to your photo with two staples at the top. No glue, no scotch tape.

- Don't list an age range. It is in the eye of the beholder anyway. I would leave off any reference to age.

- If you are free-lancing, or if you don't have representation yet, be sure to include contact info on the resume. However, women might want to leave off the

JONATHAN SLAFF

AEA - SAG - AFTRA
Ht.: 5'11''   Wt: 165   Eyes: Blue
Hair: Brown   Voice: Baritone

SERVICE: (212) 244-4270
Commercials please contact:
DON BUCHWALD & ASSOCIATES
10 East 44th Street NYC
10017
(212) 867-1070

NEW YORK THEATRE	Die Kleine Esther	Eliz. Swados, Dir.
	The Men's Group	ELT @ Linc. Ctr.
	Imag. Coming Dead	Theatre New City
	Atonements	''
	Marathon '33	Lion Theatre
	End as a Man	''
SUMMER STOCK	Make a Million	Kenley Players
	Heaven Can Wait	''
	The Merry Widow	''
	Kismet	''
FILMS	Beer	
	Zelig	
	So Fine	

TELEVISION   Something Smells Sushi (pilot)
              The Executive Crunch (syndicated)
              TV's Greatest Commercials
              60 Minutes
              One Life to Live
              All My Children
              As the World Turns
              Another World
              Joe Franklin Show

INDUSTRIAL   Matthew Bender Company
FILMS   (awards: Houston Int'l Film Fest., Industrial Film Fest.)

COMMERCIALS   Reel available upon request.

TRAINING   Acting: Wynn Handman, Bob McAndrew, Stella Adler, Jack Waltzer
              Musical Theatre: David Craig, Albert Hague
              Singing: Harry Garland
              Stage Combat: Richard Coyne
              Dance: Jerri Lines, Kathy Burke

SPECIAL   Serious & Comedic Hand-to-Hand Combat, FLUENT GERMAN, Swimming,
SKILLS   Military Drill & Manual of Arms, Horseback Riding, Skiing,
              Motorcycle & Truck Driving, Tennis, Golf, CPR, Fly & Surf
              Casting.

EDUCATION   BA Yale (history)
              MBA Columbia

home address—you never know who might pull your photo out of a trash can somewhere.

- When mailing photos and resumes, don't bother putting cardboard in the envelope. It only adds weight and doesn't prevent damage anyway.

- Want to give the impression of recent activity? Leave off a couple of credits when you type up the resume, and then write them in on each copy. It will look like you've been so busy working that you haven't had time to type up a new resume. Everybody wants a winner, remember?

- Get a personal logo for yourself, and use it on your resume if you don't have an agent's logo to put there. Wonderful and inexpensive work is being done these days in copy centers and print shops that utilize laser printers. You can put the same logo on your stationery and note pads, creating an identity for yourself.

- Note the "commercials" category on the sample resume. The actor wrote in "reel available on request" instead of listing products. You can also write "conflicts on request," (see **conflicts** in glossary) and you may want to list a few advertising agencies you have worked with. Never list products, however, because a campaign may be dead and still be carried on your resume, costing you possible auditions.

13

Performers' Unions

Before there were performers' unions, there were two categories of actors: stars and everybody else. The stars were always well-paid and coddled because they sold tickets. All the other players were considered to be interchangeable. If one didn't work out, there was another one behind the next tree. It was a classic case of supply outstripping demand, and it kept pay scales low and exploitation levels high.

Today, we still have an imbalance in supply and demand, but thanks to the unions, some dignity has been brought to the working, non-star actor. Now we have acceptable wage scales, pension plans, health insurance, dental coverage, and safety standards on sets and stages. We get residuals when our performances are sold again and again on television.

There are three primary performers' unions for you to be concerned with:

Screen Actors Guild

SAG's jurisdiction includes motion pictures, most prime-time television, most television commercials, most industrial/corporate films, and anything else that might be shot on film instead of videotape. Currently, there are about 60,000 members of this important union.

American Federation Of Television And Radio Artists

AFTRA has jurisdiction over about 10 percent of the TV commercials, all radio commercials, all live television shows such as newscasts, all soap operas, some industrial/corporate films, and anything else that might be shot on videotape instead of film. Currently, there are about 62,000 members.

Actors' Equity Association

"Equity" covers live stage performances, period. It was the first union, the granddaddy, formed in 1913 by 112 actors who were braver than us all. Currently, there are about 39,000 members, mostly in New York.

The time will surely come when SAG and AFTRA will be merged into a single union. The merger talks are now at a fever pitch, and timetables are actually in place. It's long overdue. I won't be surprised to see the day come when there will be a single union for all of the creative crafts, including directors, writers, and actors. Negotiations with producers get tougher each year. We don't deal with Sam Goldwyn anymore. Now, it's General Electric, Capital Cities, Coca-Cola, and Gulf & Western, huge conglomerates. Artists must unite.

Until then, you'll have to deal with several different unions, and they all have different forms. SAG and Equity are national unions with branches around the country; AFTRA is actually a series of local unions joined together in a Federation. It's a pain in the neck, but be glad we have the unions at all.

The Taft-Hartley Act, passed by Congress in the late Forties, set up the mechanism by which most people enter the unions. That act says that if an employer (whether a meat packer or a movie studio) has a union shop and wants to hire a person who is not in the union, then that person is allowed to work for thirty days under that union's jurisdiction without having to join the union. If he continues in the job for longer than thirty days, then he must join the union; if he works the thirty days and doesn't get an offer to stay at work, then it is his option whether he wants to join or not.

What this means is that if a producer has signed an agreement with SAG (or AFTRA or Equity) which allows him to employ union members, and he wants to hire an actor who is not yet in the union, then that actor must be allowed to join the union. He doesn't *have* to join if he doesn't want to until thirty days are up, but he can if he wants to. In even plainer English, if you go to a commercial, movie, or stage audition and wind up with the job, you can take your contract to the union office and join up.

One alternative is joining AFTRA, which has an open-door policy. You walk in, pay your money, and walk out with an AFTRA card. You will be eligible to join all of the other unions one year from that date, just as long as you have at least one job as a principal on an AFTRA production during the year. An "under five" on a soap will do the trick.

It is expensive. The current fee to join Equity is $500, SAG is $838.50, and AFTRA is $632.50. Be glad you don't want to be a movie director: it costs $5,000 to join the Directors Guild of America.

I remember being terribly frustrated and defensive about my inability to get into the unions when I first started out. One of the first questions asked by every casting director and agent was "Are you in the unions?" I would mutter something about "not yet" and hope they wouldn't hold it against me. Then, one fine day I got cast, and all my union problems ended. I was in, a pro! I share this with you so you'll know you aren't alone. Nobody was born with a union card. They have to be earned. If you really want to pursue a career as a professional actor, you'll get into the unions, all of them. I guarantee it.

14

"What Do *You* Think?"
Questions and Opinions

In no particular order, and with no particular categorization, I offer the following commonly-asked questions, along with my opinions.

Is there anything special I should be doing as a minority performer? Probably. Though we've come a long way since the Fifties, we have miles to go before we sleep. According to SAG, blacks, Latinos, Asians, and American Indians account for about 22 percent of the nation's population, but make up only 13 percent of the on-camera appearances in film, TV, and commercials (1987 stats). Most of the unions have affirmative action programs for urging producers to cast minorities, even giving them incentives to do so. You might consider contacting a local union office to see if you can add your voice to the chorus. Also, if you ask around in the theatrical community, you'll probably discover independent associations of performers who have banded together to send photos and mailings to casting directors and producers on an organized basis.

How do I stay in touch with my agent? Drop by now and then. Show him your new haircut, or take him a box of fortune cookies. Particularly early on in your relationship, you want to be visible, not just a name on a list. Telephone calls are pretty much of a waste of time, even though I know some agents who encourage their clients to "check in" this way. I think they tell you that to keep you from dropping by. Your agent is busy, or should be, and you don't want to monopolize his time, so use good judgment if you visit the office. Drop by, say "hello," and leave. If you are there for fifteen minutes, that's too long.

What kind of training should I have? How can I find good instructors? The answer to the first part is that you should have as broad an education as possible. There is no such thing as a good dumb actor. Read deeply in history, philosophy, and literature. I tell my students that I would rather see them reading the *New York Times* or a book by Hemingway than another tome on acting technique. Actors are artists and should have something to say. Get a university education if you can. If my daughter wanted to be an actress, I would advise her to complete college and then try to get into a place like Juilliard for intense, broad-based training in acting skills.

Once in the field, by all means, find a good scene-study workshop, and stay in it. Singing and dancing classes are good, as are improv workshops. If you have never done commercials, a commercial-auditioning workshop is a must. Hollywood is full of "film acting" classes, and they are fine just as long as you realize that you are studying technique. If you have never had any acting training, pure scene study is far better than a "film acting" workshop.

To find good instructors, talk to fellow actors to see who they like. As with the poll you did when searching for photographers, you'll hear the same names keep popping up. Most legitimate teachers will permit you to audit, and that is the best thing to do.

One word of caution to those who live in cities other than New York and L.A.: it is not uncommon to find yourself sitting across the desk from a franchised agent who also owns and operates an acting school. Some of them may be excellent, but tread carefully. Watch out for agents who want to "develop" you at their school or who offer a quid pro quo. ("I'll represent you if you enroll in the classes we offer"). It just might be the case that you are looking at a person who is more in the school business than the agenting business and is using the fact that he is an agent to lure prospective students. Though good training is a critical part of becoming a professional actor, when you are interviewing with agents, you should be looking for representation, not classes. It is one thing for an agent to advise you to go get some acting training and to perhaps suggest some classes to check out, but it is quite another if he is offering a six month or one year ''comprehensive program of acting training'' himself. Caveat emptor.

Finally, I pass along advice that was given to me once by a very fine actor, Conrad Bain. At a time when I was considering leaving the business for earnest work, he said to me: ''For every actor I have known who has not made it because he hasn't had the big break, I can name ten who have had the big break and weren't ready for it.'' So, whatever you do, stay in training. Be ready.

Should I do extra work? You'll get conflicting advice on this. If you are in Hollywood, I vote no. If in New York, maybe. If anywhere else, it's okay to do it now and then, but don't put it on your resume. The main problem is that a steady diet of work as an extra can take a toll on your ego. I honestly believe that one of the keys to getting cast is the conviction that you *should* be cast, that you are good enough to carry a lead role, and it's hard to feel that way about yourself if you are working on a set where you are a coat size.

Should I move to Los Angeles? New York? These two cities certainly dominate the entertainment industry today, and if you are serious about making a career of it, you should consider a move. Which place is better? I've lived in both, and my perception is that New York is a story about the legitimate theater and art; Hollywood is a story about movies, TV, and money. Wherever you go, I urge you not to do it halfheartedly. Make the move, and make a serious commitment. At minimum, give it a good three- to five-year effort.

If you are just starting on your career, however, you can build a handsome resume right where you are, and my advice is to do that before going to either New York or

Hollywood. Act in plays and student films at local colleges. Do some industrial films. You'll be in a better place if you already have a resume when you make the big move.

What about casting director showcases? Are they worthwhile? These functions take place primarily in New York and Hollywood, and are among the most controversial in the industry. The problem is that actors should not have to pay for auditions, and some of the showcases make it seem like you are doing precisely that. Even if you call them workshops or classes, how can you avoid the audition aspect? The person you are paying *is* a casting director, and he *is* forming an opinion about your work. If it looks like a duck and walks like a duck. . . .

If you are bound and determined to showcase in this fashion, then do it with your eyes wide open. Make sure that your audition techniques are already top-drawer, absolutely competitive, *before* doing the showcases. Get some training and *then* showcase. That way, you'll be getting the biggest bang for the buck.

How do I avoid being typecast? Won't it ruin my career? You have to have a career to ruin first. The truth is that it is desirable to be typed at the start of your career—at least that way they know what to do with you. My advice is to take any work you can get and worry about shaping your career later.

Casting notices in the trade papers always specify "no calls and no visits." Is that true? From the casting director's perspective, yes. From your perspective, maybe. If you believe you are right for a role, I advocate doing everything in your power to be auditioned for it. If they don't respond to a mailing quickly, then call or visit. As long as you are friendly and professional about it, no one can fault you for trying to sell your services.

Any suggestions about how to support myself while hunting for acting work? A book could be written about the strange and wonderful ways in which actors have supported themselves while "between engagements." The problem is that you rarely get more than twenty-four hours' notice of auditions, and usually it is less than that. It is common to get a call at 10:30 AM for a 2:30 PM audition. In other words, you have to be able to spin on a dime. This can be a major problem for people who are already entrenched in good-paying real-world jobs. Should I quit my job, they think, or should I just call in sick when I get an audition? Conventional jobs for Fortune 500 companies usually aren't the kind that you can pop in and out of when that exciting reading for a Pampers commercial suddenly comes up. Most mainstream employers just aren't sensitive to the artistic urge, yet you absolutely must be available for auditions when they happen; agents and casting directors will quickly stop calling you if you can't get there. I worked for a year or so as a desk clerk in a women's hotel in New York, midnight until 7:00 in the morning, just so I could have my days free. The aspiring actor who is working at Macy's has become almost a joke—everybody, it seems, has worked there at one time or another. Waiting tables and parking cars is good. The best thing is to be self-employed so you have more control over your hours, but if that isn't possible, look at seasonal jobs, food-service jobs such as catering, night-shift employment, temp jobs. A lot of actors work commission-only sales jobs because they can call their hours their own.

What about overexposure in commercials? You should be so lucky.

Conclusion

Say this out loud right now: "I am an actor."

How did it feel? Odd? *Are* you an actor? Or do you hope to be one someday?

Just because you may not have earned one red cent from acting yet does not mean that you are not an actor. They say that Picasso painted over 1,000 paintings before he ever sold one. Was he any more an artist at number 1,000 than he was at 999? Was Vincent Van Gogh less of an artist because he never sold any?

Artistry is a state of mind, a determination to communicate, and it is important for you to acknowledge your art. You need not torture yourself for not having worked as much as you think you should have. It only means you are normal.

In the same year that Babe Ruth set the record for the most home runs hit, he also held the record for the most strike-outs.

Remember that.

Appendix

AFTRA Branch Offices

5150 North 16th Street, #C-255
Phoenix, AZ 85016
602-279-9975

6922 Hollywood Boulevard
8th floor
Hollywood, CA 90028
213-461-8111

3045 Rosecrans Street, #308
San Diego, CA 92110
619-222-1161

100 Bush Street
16th floor
San Francisco, CA 94104
415-391-7510

950 South Cherry Street, #502
Denver, CO 80222
303-757-6226

20401 NW 2nd Avenue, #102
Miami, FL 33169
305-652-4824

1627 Peachtree Street NE, #210
Atlanta, GA 30309
404-897-1335

307 North Michigan Avenue
Chicago, IL 60601
312-372-8081

2475 Canal Street, #108
New Orleans, LA 70119
504-822-6568

11 Beacon Street, #512
Boston, MA 02108
617-742-2688

Highland House
5480 Wisconsin Avenue, #201
Chevy Chase, MD 20815
301-657-2560

28690 Southfield Road
Lathrup Village, MI 48076
313-559-9540

15 South 9th Street, #400
Minneapolis, MN 55402
612-371-9120

906 Olive Street, #1006
St. Louis, MO 63101
314-231-8410

260 Madison Avenue
7th floor
New York, NY 10016
212-532-0800

1367 East 6th Street, #229
Cleveland, OH 44114
216-781-2255

230 South Broad Street
10th floor
Philadelphia, PA 10192
215-732-0507

1108 17th Avenue South
Nashville, TN 37212
615-327-2944

2650 Fountainview, #325
Houston, TX 77057
713-972-1806

Two Dallas Communications
   Complex
6309 North O'Connor Road,
   #111-LB25
Irving, TX 75039
214-869-9400

601 Valley Street, #200
Seattle, WA 98109
206-282-2506

Equity Branch Offices

6430 Sunset Blvd.
Los Angeles, CA 90028
213-462-2234

100 Bush Street
16th floor
San Francisco, CA 94104
415-391-7510

203 North Wabash Avenue
Chicago, IL 60601
312-641-0393

165 West 46th Street
New York, NY 10036
212-869-8530

SAG Branch Offices

5150 North 16th Street, #C-255
Phoenix, AZ 85016
602-279-9975

7065 Hollywood Boulevard
Hollywood, CA 90028
213-465-6500

3045 Rosecrans Street, #308
San Diego, CA 92110
619-222-3996

100 Bush Street
16th floor
San Francisco, CA 94104
415-391-7510

950 South Cherry Street, #502
Denver, CO 80222
303-757-6226

2299 Douglas Road, Suite West
Miami, FL 33145
305-444-7677

1627 Peachtree Street NE, #210
Atlanta, GA 30309
404-897-1335

949 Kapiolani Boulevard, #105
Honolulu, HI 96814
808-538-6122

307 North Michigan Avenue
Chicago, IL 60601
312-372-8081

2475 Canal Street, #108
New Orleans, LA 70119
504-822-6568

11 Beacon Street, #512
Boston, MA 02108
617-742-2688

Highland House
5480 Wisconsin Avenue, #201
Chevy Chase, MD 20815
301-657-2560

28690 Southfield Road
Lathrup Village, MI 48076
313-559-9540

15 South 9th Street, #400
Minneapolis, MN 55402
612-371-9120

906 Olive Street, #1006
St. Louis, MO 63101
314-231-8410

1515 Broadway
44th floor
New York, NY 10036
212-944-1030

1367 East 6th Street, #229
Cleveland, OH 44114
216-579-9305

230 South Broad Street
10th floor
Philadelphia, PA 10192
215-545-3150

1108 17th Avenue South
Nashville, TN 37212
615-327-2958

2650 Fountainview, #325
Houston, TX 77057
713-972-1806

Two Dallas Communications
    Complex
6309 North O'Connor Road,
    #111-LB25
Irving, TX 75039
214-869-9400

601 Valley Street, #200
Seattle, WA 98109
206-282-2506

Glossary

Academy Players Directory   The West Coast equivalent of New York's Player's Guide. For a fee, you can get your photo and contact numbers listed here. Producers, casting directors, and agents use it for reference.

A.D.   Assistant Director. On a film or TV set, there is usually a First A.D. and one or more Second A.D.s. They keep things organized, tell the extras which way to move, and so on. In general terms, the A.D. in films is equivalent to a **stage manager** in theater except that an A.D. is usually serious about becoming an actual director. It is a stepping-stone position. A First A.D. outranks a Second A.D.

ad agency   The creative nerve center of commercials. The concepts originate here, and the actual production is subcontracted to **production houses.**

ADR   Automatic Dialogue Replacement. Now that computers have entered the picture, this is the new name for **looping.**

AEA   Actors' Equity Association. The union that covers the legitimate stage only. No film or TV. Actors and stage managers are both members of Equity.

AFTRA   The American Federation of TV and Radio Artists is a performers' union that covers all radio, all live TV, most TV shows recorded on videotape like game shows, variety shows, soap operas, and most corporate films.

agent   The actor's representative in the marketplace. The distinction to keep in mind is that some agents are **franchised**—approved by the unions to represent union talent—and some are not. Even if you aren't in the union, you need a franchised agent. The agent collects 10 percent of your earnings as his fee.

AGMA   Associated Guild of Musical Artists. One of the affiliated performers' unions.

AGVA   Associated Guild of Variety Artists. Another of the affiliated performers' unions.

animatic   A kind of quasi-commercial that ad agencies sometimes employ to show a client the general idea of a campaign. They shoot a series of stills with a regular SLR camera and then videotape them so that, when the tape is replayed, there is a feeling of animation. If the client likes the animatic, the agency might go ahead and make a full production spot.

ANNCR or V/O   Announcer or Voice Over. Usually refers to an off-camera performer who records his part in a sound studio. Later, it is mechanically edited into the film. You see these abbreviations a lot in commercial scripts. V/O could also refer to what we hear while a picture of something else is on the screen. A commercial might start out with a performer on camera and then, as the camera pans to a product shot, we still hear the performer talking. On the script, that would be indicated as: "Performer V/O."

apron   On a proscenium stage, this is the frontal lip of the stage, the part closest to the audience.

art director   The person who designs sets, usually on commercials.

ATA   Association of Talent Agents.

availability   In commercials, after final auditions, the producer may specify a potential time span for the shoot and ask for your "availability." If you get an offer for another job during that time, you should tell him, so he can book you first if he wants to. It is all a courtesy and has no legal status at all: it doesn't mean you are going to get paid.

best boy   On film sets, the best boy is an assistant to the **gaffer** and helps handle all the equipment.

blue sky   A film term that involves camera and editing tricks. They might shoot an actual burning building, for example, and then later film the firemen running up and down a ladder in a parking lot somewhere with the ''blue sky'' behind them. Then, in the editing room, the two shots are put together to make it seem like the firemen were actually at the site of the fire.

book   As in ''Could I see your book, Bob?'' Otherwise known as a portfolio, all models carry these around as they go to interviews. Actors who have impressive collections of stills from past shows (''This is me as Portia . . . '') sometime like to have a book, but it is certainly not necessary.

booking   As in ''You have a booking, Bob.'' You only hear this term in commercials and modeling, never in theater. It means you got the job. If they cancel after this, you still get a session fee.

boom   An overhead microphone, usually held on a long pole.

callback   After the first audition, they have narrowed down the field to a few promising candidates, of which you are one. That means you have a callback. It is a second, third, or fourth audition.

call sheet   On a film or TV show, this is prepared daily by the production office and is a handy thing to have. Among other info, it contains a list of the actors who are working the next day and tells what their call times are. You can get one from the **A.D.**

call time   This is what time you are supposed to report to the set on a film, TV show, or commercial. When you get there, check in with the **A.D.**

camera left   The actor's right as he faces the camera.

camera right   The actor's left as he faces the camera.

card   A term you'll hear when your agent is negotiating your billing on a film or TV show. Your name might appear alone on the screen (''separate card'') or with others (''shared card'').

casting director   Works for the producer and has the job of finding appropriate actors to audition for the roles.

client   The company that pays the bills in commercials. If you are doing a spot for Pampers, then Proctor & Gamble is the client.

commission   A percentage of a performer's earnings paid to agents or managers for services rendered.

composite   A two-sided composition of photos used almost exclusively by actors who do commercials. The front usually displays a headshot, and the reverse contains four or five situational shots that show how you can be cast. Not to be confused with a **headshot** or a **zed card**.

conflicts   As in ''Do you have any conflicts with Pepsi, Bob?'' Union rules say that you can't have two commercials for the same kind of product running at the same time. You can't have a Pepsi and a Coke spot simultaneously. If you get caught with conflicting products on the air, you can get sued for production costs. It's not worth it.

corporate film   See **industrial/educational film.**

cross   Definitely not a religious term. It means that the actor is supposed to cross from one place to another on the set. As in ''You'll make your cross on your next line, Bob.''

CSA   The Casting Society of America.

cue   This is the line immediately before yours. A cue can also be non-verbal. ''Your cue is when the phone rings, Bob.''

cue card   A piece of white poster board used in commercial auditions which the casting director writes the copy with a magic marker. He puts it on a stand next to the camera so you can refer to it instead of holding the script in your hand. SAG requires cue cards at auditions.

day player   An actor who is hired for one day on a movie or TV show.

day-out-of-days   A term your agent will use when negotiating your shooting schedule on a TV show or movie—how many days you will work out of the total production schedule of days.

dealer spot   A type of commercial in which the dealers that sell a particular advertised product all toss some money into a pot and have their names tagged on to the spot. You see this a lot with commercials for cars and house paints.

dolly   When they move the camera toward you or away from you during a shot, that's called ''dollying.'' This is different from "zooming," where the camera stays in one place and the lens is shifted for a closeup shot.

downgrade When they hire you as a principal performer in a commercial, but your footage winds up on the cutting-room floor, they will downgrade you from a principal to an extra. No residuals.

downstage This is in front of the actor as he is standing on the stage facing the audience.

ECU An abbreviation for Extreme Close-up. Typically seen in film, TV, and commercial scripts, this term refers to a tight shot of something.

Equity See **Actors' Equity Association.**

Equity principal interview See **open call.**

EXT An abbreviation for Exterior; a scene that is shot outside.

first refusal In commercials, after final auditions, the producer may ask you for "first refusal." As with **availability**, this is a courtesy and not a binding agreement. What he wants is the right to hire you before you accept a conflicting assignment.

first-run syndication Describes television programs that are produced for and sold to independent TV stations all across the country; this is an alternative to selling a show to one of the three networks which would, in turn, feed the programming to its affiliates.

foley To enhance individual sound effects on film. The sound of footsteps on loose gravel, for example, might be enhanced to sound more ominous. Richard Gere and Debra Winger's kissing scenes in *An Officer And A Gentleman* were treated this way, a fact I can never seem to forget when I watch the movie. The people who do this work are specialists known as Foley Artists.

four A's Associated Actors and Artistes of America, the umbrella organization for AFTRA, SAG, and other performers' unions. You always hear it referred to as "four A's," never as "AAAA."

franchise When an agent signs up with the unions, he is franchised, i.e., approved to represent union talent.

gaffer The chief electrician on a film set.

golden time On a TV or movie set, this refers to overtime after the 16th hour. It is golden because your pay starts skyrocketing.

half-hour   Your **call time** in the theatre. Literally, it means you should be there a half hour before the curtain goes up.

headshot   Another name for an 8 x 10 glossy photo, not to be confused with a **composite** or a **zed card.**

honey wagon   Dressing room on wheels. You get assigned one of your own when you are working on a TV show or movie. It's called a Honey Wagon because the accompanying toilets can be aromatic.

IATSE   International Alliance of Theatrical Stage Employees and Motion Picture Machine Operators of the United States and Canada. This is one of the two unions that represent editors, camera operators, electricians, set designers, and other crafts workers on movies and TV shows. The other union is NABET. It is said that IATSE people may be a little better qualified, but the union is stodgy and given to cronyism.

industrial/educational film   Also known as a **corporate film**, this is made by a business for use in training or motivating its employees.

industrial show   A live Las Vegas/Broadway-style sales extravaganza, staged by a company, complete with singers and dancers.

INT   Interior; a scene shot inside as opposed to outside.

interactive video   A new kind of **industrial/educational film** that allows the viewer to interact with what is happening on the screen. It is the product of a marriage between the video-disc and the personal computer.

key grip   The person on a film set who helps set up the camera, as well as the dolly it sits on.

League of American Theaters and Producers   The national association of theatrical producers and theater operators.

location   When you are not shooting on a soundstage, you ''go on location.''

loop   Also known as **automatic dialogue replacement**. This is what you do when you go into a recording studio, watch film (usually of yourself), and simultaneously record dialogue so that it is in sync with the moving lips on the screen. Sometimes this is necessary because the sound may have been improperly recorded during filming. Perhaps there was unwanted background noise, so they make a clean sound track and ''loop'' the dialogue.

LORT Acronym for League of Resident Theatres, a national organization of not-for-profit theaters. Equity has a LORT contract.

manager A person who contractually "manages" a performer's overall career. The usual fee for this service is 15 percent of what you earn. Not to be confused with an **agent.**

mark The spot, usually indicated with a piece of tape on the ground, where the actor is supposed to stand when "action" is called.

M.O.S. An abbreviation for "mit out sound" (without sound). This means they are recording picture, but no sound. The origin of the term goes back to the early days of Hollywood, when there were a lot of German movie directors who couldn't speak English well. Some say Lothar Mendes, some say Eric Von Stroheim was the one to coin it. Whoever it was, it stuck as an industry term. You'll see it written on the slate.

NABET National Association of Broadcast Employees and Technicians. One of the two unions that represent camera operators and other crafts on movies and TV shows. The other one is IATSE.

name slug See **slug.**

NATPE Acronym for National Association of Television Program Executives. The annual NATPE conference is where producers of shows intended for first-run syndication display their wares to buyers from TV stations across the country.

NATR The National Association of Talent Representatives (New York only).

non-Equity A non-Equity or non-union stage production is one that may not employ union members. There is pay involved, but it generally will not come up to union minimums, and you won't encounter such niceties as pension and welfare contributions. Don't confuse non-Equity shows with Equity waiver.

no quote A term used in TV to indicate that you are receiving less than your usual rate, or "quote," for an acting job, but everybody promises not to tell.

O/C On Camera. Refers to whatever the camera is seeing, be it a person, place or thing.

open call Known more formally as an Equity principal interview or, on the street, as a cattle call, this is where the casting process is theoretically thrown open to all comers. You get to hand your picture to a representative of the production, who makes a decision about whether or not you should get a subsequent audition.

P.A.   Production Assistant, a fancy word for a gofer.

pan   A camera shot which sweeps from side to side, as in ''We'll pan with you when you drive by on your bike, Bob.''

per diem   When you work on location, this is a fee paid by the producer to compensate for the cost of meals not provided by the producer. In other words, if you have to eat in restaurants, they pay for it.

pick up   When a take gets botched while filming, you might do a ''pick up,'' starting in the middle of the scene. It has nothing whatever to do with bars.

Players' Guide   The New York equivalent of Hollywood's Academy Players Directory. For a fee, you can list your photo and contact numbers here. Consulted by producers, casting directors, and agents.

post-production   Everything that takes place on a TV show, movie, or commercial after shooting is completed. Editing, for example, is a post-production activity.

pre-production   Everything that takes place on a TV show, movie, or commercial before shooting commences. Casting, for example, is a pre-production activity.

pre-screen   The casting director wants to check you out before you read for the producer and director, so she pre-screens you. It might involve a cold reading, the opportunity to present prepared monologues, or just a meeting.

prime time   Network programming aired 8:00 to 11:00 PM (7:00 to 10:00 PM in Central/Mountain time zones).

production house   The ad agency subcontracts the actual production of a commercial to a production house. Usually, a director comes attached to a production house.

quote   Your rate, how much you get paid for TV and film.

reel   A videotaped composite of excerpts from your film, TV, or commercial work, usually on a 3/4-inch format. Some actors have several different reels, one for film/TV, another for corporate/industrial, and yet another for commercials. You use the reel as an extension of your headshot and composite. It is just another way to let potential employers see your work.

reverse   As in "Okay, Bob, let's get a reverse on that." Refers to moving the camera around to shoot the other actor's point of view.

SAG   Screen Actors Guild, the largest of the performers' unions. Its jurisdiction includes motion pictures, most TV shows, (those that are filmed rather than videotaped), and many corporate films.

SEG   Screen Extras Guild. One of the affiliated performers' unions. SEG represents extras on the West Coast only; SAG has jurisdiction over extras in New York, Philadelphia, Boston, Baltimore, and Washington, D.C.

set   Where performers do their work, as in "When you get out of makeup, I'll take you to the set, Bob."

set-up   When they move the camera, lights, etc. from the kitchen set to the bathroom set, that change involves a new set-up. A term used in film.

SFX   Sound effects, like the sound of a door closing, the sound of coffee being poured, the sound of a distant drum, and so on.

sides   Pages from a movie or TV script that have been excerpted for the purposes of auditions.

signator   A producer who has signed an agreement with a union, thereby enabling him to employ union talent.

single   See **two-shot.**

slate   To look into the lens of the camera and say who you are. As in "Slate your name, please." Used in commercial casting. Also, a device (sometimes called "sticks") used to indicate which scene and shot is being recorded. Most often, it looks like a little chalk board, and they take a picture of it just before calling "action!"

slug   When you have your name put on your 8 x 10 glossy, they are dropping in a slug.

soundstage   A soundproof building used for shooting movies, TV shows, or commercials.

spike   Fluorescent tape used in theater. It is put on the lips of steps and other protrusions so you can see where you are going in the dark.

stage left   The actor's left as he stands on the stage facing the audience.

stage manager   The director's right-hand person in the theater, he is in charge of running the show once it opens.

stage right   The actor's right as he stands on the stage facing the audience.

Station 12   When you are hired to do a commercial, the casting director checks with **SAG** to be sure you are eligible to work. The department at SAG that handles cast-clearance of this type is known as Station 12. If you aren't up to date with your dues, for example, Station 12 will know about it and tell the casting director.

sticks   See **slate.**

storyboard   A cartoon depiction of what the commercial or movie is going to look like on a shot-by-shot basis. Looks a lot like the Sunday comics except it is in black and white.

take   The period of time the camera is actually rolling, the time between "Action!" and "Cut!"

teleprompter   A device in which the script is typed on a long roll of paper and then slowly scrolled during performance for the performer's reference. Used on newscasts, some talk shows, soap operas, and some corporate films. You don't see this on a movie set or in auditions.

test commercial   A commercial made to run in a very limited market, usually one city. If the product sells there, the spot might be "rolled out" to a broader market.

three bells   On a soundstage, three loud, prolonged rings of a bell means a scene is about to be shot, and everybody should be quiet. One loud ring means you can talk again.

top-of-the-show   A common term in the TV industry that indicates an unofficial but firm salary ceiling, beyond which the producers theoretically will not negotiate. If you're cast on a sitcom in a guest-star role, you will likely be paid "top-of-the-show," probably no more than $1,600 for the episode. Your agent would be unable to negotiate above that.

track   To move the camera along metal tracks laid down so the camera can **dolly** smoothly, as in "We'll track along with you as you walk to the car, Bob."

traffic department If you want to know where your commercial is running so your mom can see it, call the ad agency and ask for the Traffic Department. They purchase air time and keep up with this kind of thing.

turnaround The number of hours between dismissal one day and **call time** the next day.

TV Q Abbreviation for TV Quotient, a controversial rating based on a survey of the recognizability and likability of TV performers conducted by Market Evaluation, Inc. in Port Washington, New York. A performer's TV Q rating can dramatically affect his or her career on TV.

two-shot As in "Okay, Bob, let's get a two-shot." It means there will be two people on camera instead of one, which would be a "single."

under five An actor who is hired to speak fewer than five lines. You hear this term a lot in the world of soap operas. Literally, it equates to no more than fifty words. Talk more than that, and you get paid more.

upstage Behind the actor as he stands on the stage facing the audience. When someone "upstages" you, he is doing something behind your back while you are facing the audience.

waiver In a nutshell, one of the unions is allowing its members to work in a particular production without being paid, or waiving wages. Equity waiver is the term used for stage, and SAG waiver normally applies to certain student films, like those made at American Film Institute, NYU, or USC. The important thing to remember about waiver is that each individual production must be approved by the union. If you are non-union, you can definitely appear in a waiver show, right alongside of union members who are waiving their pay.

Walla Crowd sounds in movies and TV shows. It is recorded in the same manner as **looping.**

WGA Writers Guild of America, the union for screenwriters.

wildspot When a commercial runs in specific cities instead of on a national basis, it is running "wildspot." The advertiser pays a set fee per city for thirteen weeks of unlimited use. It is possible, even probable, that a spot will run both network and wildspot at the same time.

wrap   The end of a production. "It's a wrap!" Sometimes they have a party after this.

zed card   A slick, frequently full-color, photo card used by professional models. Actors have no need for this at all.

Index

Accents, use of, 16–17
Acting
    as art form, 78–79
    for movies, 83–85
    as reacting, 84–85
    on stage, 84
Acting career, managing your,
        107–10
Acting schools operated by fran-
        chised agents, 138–39
Actors
    relationship between casting
        directors and, 21–22
    type categories of, 115–16
Actors' Equity Association (AEA),
        112, 135, 136, 146
Ad agency, instructions for TV
    commercial from, 40
Advertisements. *See* Commercials,
    auditoning for; Radio
    commercials; TV commercials
Advertising claims, 52–53, 54
AFTRA, 59, 61, 88, 112, 135, 136
    branch offices, 145–46
Age, resume and, 130, 131
Agents, 109, 111–23
    casting for corporate films by, 92
    changing, 121–22
    commercial, 112, 113, 115, 118
    exclusivity versus free-lance
        representation, 120–21
    franchised agencies, 20–21, 112,
        113, 138–39
    full-service, 112, 113, 118
    hints for finding and keeping,
        122–23
    Hollywood vs. New York, 112,
        120, 122
    how they work, 112–13
    interview with, 118–20
        setting up, 113–14, 122–23

    making contact with, 113–18
    new, 117–118
    questions to ask before audition,
        102–4
    theatrical, 113, 115, 118, 119–20
    type categories of actors, 115–16
    ways to stay in touch with, 129,
        137–138
American Federation of Television
        and Radio Artists (AFTRA),
        59, 61, 88, 112, 135, 136
    branch offices, 145–46
Anxiety, audition, 7–13
    practical exercises to manage,
        12–13
    self-fulfilling prophecy and,
        10–12
    symptoms of, 8–10
Appearance, physical, 18–19, 118.
        See also Clothes
"Aside" in TV commercial, 38
Audition, notice of, 140
Audition checklist, 102–4

Billing, TV show, 74–75
Budget, TV vs. movie, 81
Business side of acting, 105–41
    agents, finding and keeping, 109,
        111–23
    management of career, 107–10
    performers' unions, 112, 134–36
    theatrical photos and resumes,
        104, 109, 113, 117, 124–33
"Button," 54

Cable television, 75, 76
Callback audition, 34, 51–52
Camera, working with videotape,
        35–39, 52, 53
Career, managing your acting,
        107–10

Cartoon voices, 16, 59
Casting
  for movies, 81–83
  for stage productions, 95–96
  for TV commercials, 34–35
  for TV shows, 63, 64–65
  for voice work, 58–59
"Casting couches," 21–22
Casting directors, 20–25
  how they work, 20–22
  independent, 35, 59, 61
  for movie, 82, 85–86
  pre-screen interviews with, 22–23
  relationship between actors and,
    21–22
  "result" direction from, 39–41
  for stage, 95–96
  TV commercial auditioning pro-
    cess and, 46–47
  for TV show, 70–71, 82
  for voice work, 58
Casting director showcases, 140
Casting notices in trade papers, 140
Character, playing a, 14–17
Checklist, audition, 102–4
Classical monologues, 99, 100
Clothes, 24, 103
  costuming for auditions, 17
  for industrial/educational film
    audition, 90
  for interview with agent, 118
  for theatrical photo, 126
  for TV commercial audition, 34–
    35, 51
Color photos, 128
Commercial agent, 112, 113, 115,118
Commercial pre-screens, 22
Commercials, auditioning for
  composites for, 127–28
  playing character for, 15–16
  questions to ask agent about,
    102–3
  See also Radio commercials; TV
    commercials
Commercial voice demo tape, 59–60
Composites, 127–28
Conflicts, 133
Corporate films. See Industrial/
    educational films
Co-star billing in TV, 74
Costuming for auditions, 17
Cue cards, 44–46

Day jobs, 119, 140–141
Demo reel, industrial, 92–93
Demo tape, commercial voice,
    59–60
Dialogue replacement, 57
Direction
  "result," 39–41
  "situational," 39–40
Directors
  at callback audition for TV com-
    mercial, 51
  movie, 82, 83, 86
  of movies-of-the-week, 82
  questions to ask agent about, 103
  at stage auditions, 95, 96–97
  TV show, 64, 69–70, 82
  See also Casting directors
Directors Guild of America, 136
Dress. See Clothes

Educational films. See Industrial/
    educational films
"End credits at producer's discre-
    tion," 75
Episodic TV shows, 66, 72–73
Equity. See Actors' Equity Associa-
    tion (AEA)
Exclusivity versus free-lance repre-
    sentation, 120–21
Extra work, 139
Eyeglasses, wearing, 19

Facial hair, 18
Fear. See Anxiety, audition
Featured billing in TV, 74, 75
Fees, union, 136
Fighting scenes, 98
File card system for records, 108–9
Films. See Industrial/educational
    films; Movies
First-run syndication, 76, 77
Food, eating, 47
Franchised agencies, 20–21, 112,
    113
  acting schools run by, 138–39
Free-lance representation versus ex-
    clusivity, 120–21
Full-service agencies, 112, 113, 118

Groups, working on videotape
    in, 38
Guest star billing in TV, 74

Guidelines, audition, 14–19
  physical appearance, 18–19
  playing a character, 14–17

Hair, appearance of, 18, 126
Headshot, theatrical, 125–27
Hollywood, 78, 117
  agents in, 112, 120, 122
  casting director showcases in, 140
  extra work in, 139
  photos for, 128
  resume format for, 130, 131
  as TV production center, 62–
    64, 77

Improvisational auditions, 42,
    48–50
Independent casting directors, 35,
    59, 61
Independent TV stations, 75–76
Industrial/educational films, 88–93
  auditioning process for, 90–91
  finding jobs in, 91–93
  future of, 93
Instructors, finding good, 138–39
Interactive video, 93
Interviews
  with agent, 118–20
    setting up, 113–14, 122–23
  pre-screen
    with casting directors, 22–25
    for stage, 95

Jobs between acting work, 119,
    140–41

Kissing scenes, 98

Logo, using personal, 133
Los Angeles
  agencies in, 112
  moving to, 139–40
  resume format for, 130, 131

Makeup, 18–19, 126–27
Male voices, domination in voice
    work by, 61
Management of acting career,
    107–10
Market research in advertising, 33
Memorizing for TV commercial,
    44–46

Men, portrayal in TV commercials
    of, 31
Microphone, working with, 56
Minority performers, 137
Mirrors, rehearsing in front of,
    43–44
Monologues, 95, 99–102, 118, 120
Motivation
  in improvisational auditions, 49
  for TV show auditions, 69, 72
Movement in stage audition, 97–98
Movie pre-screens, 22–23
Movies, 78–87
  acting for, 83–85
  budget for, 81
  casting directors for, 82, 85–86
  casting for, 81–83
  directors of, 82, 83, 86
  future of, 86–87
  hints for auditioning for, 85–86
  similarities between stage and, 80
Movies-of-the-week, 73, 82
Moving to New York or Los An-
    geles, 139–40
Multiplex theaters, 86, 87

Names of auditors, remembering,
    104
Narration jobs, 61
Networking for voice work, 57–
    58, 59
Networks, TV, 75–77
New York
  agents in, 112
    "making rounds" of, 117, 120
  casting director showcases in, 140
  extra work in, 139
  moving to, 139–40
  photos for, 128
  resume format for, 130, 132
Non-actors in TV commercials, 29–
    30, 112

Office space, need for, 108
One- and two-line roles, 72

Pace of scene, controlling, 70–71
Pace of work on TV shows, 62,
    64–65
Pay rate on TV, 74–75
Performers' unions, 112, 134–36,
    137

Personalizing the videotape camera, 36–38
Personal logo, using, 133
Photographers, 125, 128
Photos, theatrical, 104, 109, 113, 114, 124–29, 131
  budget for, 128–29
  composites, 127–28
  headshot, 125–27
  postcards, 129
  repackaging oneself with new, 116
Physical appearance, 18–19, 118. *See also* Clothes
Physicality in stage auditions, 98
Pilots, TV, 73
Planning, long-range career, 109–10
Playing a character, 14–17
Postcards, 129
Pre-screen interview
  with casting directors, 22–25
  for stage, 95
Producers
  corporate film, 88–89
  voice demo tape, 60
Products, handling, 47
Publications, trade, 109, 117, 140

"Quote" (pay rate), 74

Radio commercials, 58
  creating character voices for, 16
"Rate," 74–75
Reacting, acting as, 84–85
Receptionists, agency, 122
Recording booth, 58
Recording studios, 56
Record-keeping system, 108–9
Rehearsal
  for TV commercial, 43–44
  for TV show, 64, 65, 66
Repackaging oneself, 116–17
Representation. *See* Agents
"Result" direction, 39–41
Resumes, theatrical, 104, 117, 129–33

Scene for agent, putting up, 120
Scene-study workshops, 138
Screen Actors Guild (SAG), 137
  branch offices, 146–47
  help with finding agent, 112, 113

joining, 136
jurisdiction of, 134–35
members' earnings from commercials, 29
rules for TV commercial auditions, 42, 44
voice work and, 59, 61
Screen tests, 83
Scripts, 91, 98, 103. *See also* Sides
Self-fulfilling prophecy, audition anxiety and, 10–12
Sense-of-life audition, 48, 50
"Separate card" billing, 75
"Shared card" billing, 75
Showcases, casting director, 140
Sides, 22–23, 63, 66–68, 83
Sitcoms, three-camera, 66
"Situational" direction, 39–40
Situational improv audition, 48–49
Soap operas, 62, 66
"Soundalike" voices, 55
"Spokesperson" role, 54
Stage, 94–104
  acting on, 84
  as actor's medium, 94
  audition checklist, 102–4
  casting for, 95–96
  director's concerns at audition for, 96–97
  hints for auditioning for, 97–99
  monologues on, 95, 99–102
  similarities between movies and, 80
Stage manager, 95, 96, 98
Stage pre-screens, 22–23
Storyboard for TV commercial, 41–42
Stress, 7–8. *See also* Anxiety, audition
Studios, movie, 86–87
Substitution, using, 90–91
Success, rehearsing, 13
Swimsuit auditions, 17
Syndication, first-run, 76, 77

Talent agents. *See* Agents
Telephone services, voice work in, 56
Tension. *See* Anxiety, audition
Theater. *See* Stage
Theatrical agent, 113, 115, 118, 119–20

Theatrical photos and resumes. *See* Photos, theatrical; Resumes, theatrical
Three-camera sitcoms, 66
Trade publications, 109, 117
  casting notices in, 140
Training, 108, 138
TV commercials, 29–54
  auditioning for
    callback audition, 34, 51–52
    clothes to wear, 34–35, 51
    handling products and eating food, 47
    hints for, 52–54
    improvisational auditions, 42, 48–50
    memorizing and cue cards, 44–46
    preparing for, 41–44
    process of, 46–47
    "result" direction and, 39–41
    SAG rule for, 42, 44
  casting of, 34–35
  life as portrayed in, 30–34
  for nonexistent test products, 33–34
  working with videotape, 34, 35–39
TV pre-screens, 22–23
TV Q, 82
TV shows, 62–77
  auditioning process, 69–72
  billing, 74–75
  budget for, 81
  casting directors for, 70–71, 82
  casting for, 63, 64–65
  directors of, 64, 69–70, 82
  episodes, pilots, and movies-of-the-week, 72–73
  future of television, 75–77
  Hollywood as production center for, 62–64, 77
  pace of work on, 62, 64–65
  portrayal of life on, 80, 81

  preparing for audition, 68–69
  rehearsal for, 64, 65, 66
  sides, 66–68
  three-camera vs. episodic vs. soap operas, 66
Typecasting, 140
Type categories of actors, 115–16

Unions, performers', 112, 134–36, 137
  See also Actors' Equity Association (AEA); American Federation of Television and Radio Artists (AFTRA); Screen Actors Guild (SAG)

Video, interactive, 93
Videocassette market, 86, 87
Videotape
  for industrial/educational film audition, 90
  for TV commercials, 34, 35–39
  for TV show auditions, 64
  working with camera, 35–39, 52, 53
Voice agents, 59, 61
Voice work, 55–61
  casting for, 58–59
  creating character voice for cartoons or radio commercials, 16
  how to get started in, 59–61
  possibilities in, 55–56
  versatility in, 56–57

Walla, 55, 57–58
Weight, appearance and, 19
Women, portrayal in TV commercials, 31, 32
Work between acting jobs, 119, 140–41
Workshops, 138
  for acting on camera, 85
  for voice work, 59, 60

About the Author

Ed Hooks has been acting in theater, film, and television for 20 years. His credits include over 100 stage plays in New York and Los Angeles; TV shows such as "Hill Street Blues," "St. Elsewhere," and "Knot's Landing"; and numerous feature films and movies-of-the-week. He has also appeared in TV commercials for more than 150 accounts, including AT & T, Ricoh Copiers, Pampers, and McDonald's.

Mr. Hooks has been teaching acting and auditioning technique for more than a decade. He currently lives in Los Angeles with his wife and daughter.